The Complete Guide to Boston Terriers

Vanessa Richie

LP Media Inc. Publishing

Text copyright © 2020 by LP Media Inc.

All rights reserved.

No part of this book may be reproduced or transmitted in any form or by any means, electronic or mechanical, including photocopying, recording, or by an information storage and retrieval system - except by a reviewer who may quote brief passages in a review to be printed in a magazine or newspaper - without permission in writing from the publisher. For information address LP Media Inc. Publishing, 3178 253rd Ave. NW, Isanti, MN 55040

www.lpmedia.org

Publication Data

Vanessa Richie

The Complete Guide to Boston Terriers ---- First edition.

Summary: "Successfully raising a Boston Terrier from puppy to old age" --- Provided by publisher.

ISBN: 978-1-952069-09-3

[1.Boston Terriers --- Non-Fiction] I. Title.

This book has been written with the published intent to provide accurate and authoritative information in regard to the subject matter included. While every reasonable precaution has been taken in preparation of this book the author and publisher expressly disclaim responsibility for any errors, omissions, or adverse effects arising from the use or application of the information contained inside. The techniques and suggestions are to be used at the reader's discretion and are not to be considered a substitute for professional veterinary care. If you suspect a medical problem with your dog, consult your veterinarian.

Design by Sorin Rădulescu

First paperback edition, 2020

TABLE OF CONTENTS

INTRODUCTION 10

CHAPTER 1
An All-American Dog 12
Their Roots As Fighters 12
The American Gentleman 13
A History Of Companionship 14

CHAPTER 2
Compact Dog With a Large Personality 16
The Defining Physical Characteristics Of The Boston Terrier 17
Health Problems Common To Boston Terriers 17
    Lots Of Genetic Issues 19
    A Warning About Allergies And Stomach Sensitivities 19
A Charming Entertainer 20
A Fantastic Dog For An Urban Home 21
A Warning About Snorting, Slobbering, And Flatulence 21

CHAPTER 3
Finding Your Boston Terrier 22
Considerations And Steps To Rescue An Adult Boston Terrier 22
    Considerations 23
    Steps To Rescuing A Boston Terrier 27
Considerations For Adopting A Puppy And Picking A Breeder 28
    Choosing A Breeder 30
    Contracts And Guarantees 32
    Health Tests And Certifications 33
    Selecting A Puppy From A Breeder 34

CHAPTER 4
Preparing Your Family ... 36
Planning The First Year's Budget ... 36
Instructing Children ... 39
    Always Be Gentle And Respectful ... 41
    Mealtime ... 41
    Chase ... 42
    Paws On The Ground ... 42
    Keep Valuables Out Of Reach ... 42
Preparing Your Current Dogs ... 43
    Stick To A Schedule ... 43
    Helping Your Dog Prepare – Extra At Home Playdates ... 44
    A Friend To Your Whole Family, Even Cats ... 45

CHAPTER 5
Preparing Your Home And Schedule ... 46
Creating A Safe Space For Your Dog Or Puppy ... 48
Getting The Right Crate ... 49
Purchase And Prepare Supplies And Tools ... 49
Puppy Proof The House ... 50
    Indoor Hazards And Fixes ... 50
    Outdoor Hazards And Fixes ... 53
Choosing Your Veterinarian ... 56

CHAPTER 6
Bringing Your Boston Terrier Home ... 58
Final Preparations And Planning ... 59
    Ensure You Have Food And Other Supplies On Hand ... 59
    Design A Tentative Puppy Schedule ... 59
    Do A Quick Final Puppy Proofing Inspection Before The Puppy Arrives ... 60
    Initial Meeting ... 60
Picking Up Your Puppy Or Dog And The Ride Home ... 60
The First Vet Visit And What To Expect ... 64
Crate And Other Preliminary Training ... 66
First Night Frights ... 68

CHAPTER 7
The Multi-Pet Household ... 70
Introducing Your New Puppy To Your Other Pets ... 70
Introducing An Adult Dog To Other Animals ... 73
Older Dogs And Your Boston Terrier ... 74

Dog Aggression And Territorial Behaviors ... 75
Strong Natural Prey Drive ... 77
Feeding Time Practices ... 78

CHAPTER 8
The First Few Weeks ... 80
Setting The Rules And Sticking To Them ... 81
Establish A No Jumping And No Mouthing Policy ... 82
- Nipping ... 82
- Chewing ... 83
- Jumping ... 84

Reward-Based Training Vs Discipline-Based Training ... 85
Separation Anxiety In Dogs And Puppies ... 86
How Long Is Too Long To Be Left Home Alone? ... 88
Don't Overdo It, Physically Or Mentally ... 89

CHAPTER 9
Housetraining ... 90
Strap In – It's Going To Be A Challenge ... 91
Inside Or Outside – Housetraining Options And Considerations ... 92
- Setting A Schedule ... 93
- Choosing A Location ... 95
- Keyword Training ... 95

Reward Good Behavior With Positive Reinforcement ... 96
Cleaning Up ... 97

CHAPTER 10
Socialization ... 98
Socialization Can Make Life Easier In The Long Run ... 99
Greeting New People ... 100
Greeting New Dogs ... 103
The Importance Of Continuing Socialization ... 103
Socializing An Adult Dog ... 104

CHAPTER 11
Training Your Boston Terrier ... 106
Benefits Of Proper Training ... 107
Choosing The Right Reward ... 107
Name Recognition ... 109
Essential Commands ... 109
- Sit ... 111

- Down … **112**
- Stay … **112**
- Come … **113**
- Off … **114**
- Leave It … **114**
- Drop It … **115**
- Quiet … **117**

Where To Go From Here … **117**
- Puppy Classes … **117**
- Obedience Training … **118**

CHAPTER 12
Nutrition … **120**

Why A Healthy Diet Is Important … **121**
Dangerous Foods … **121**
Canine Nutrition … **122**
- Proteins And Amino Acids … **124**
- Fat And Fatty Acids … **125**
- Carbohydrates And Cooked Foods … **126**

Different Dietary Requirements For Different Life Stages … **126**
- Puppy Food … **126**
- Adult Dog Food … **126**
- Senior Dog Food … **127**

Your Dog's Meal Options … **128**
Scheduling Meals … **132**
Food Allergies And Intolerance … **133**

CHAPTER 13
An Entertainer Who Is Game For Fun Around The Home … **134**

Exercise Needs … **135**
A Wide, Easy Activity Range … **137**
- Fetch … **137**
- In The Sprinkler … **137**
- Agility Training … **138**

Playtime! And More Playtime! … **138**

CHAPTER 14
Grooming – Productive Bonding … **140**

Grooming Tools … **140**
Coat Management … **141**

Puppies	141
Adult Dogs	141
Senior Dogs	142
Allergies	142
Bath Time	142
Cleaning Eyes And Ears	146
Trimming Nails	147
Oral Health And Brushing Your Dog's Teeth	148

CHAPTER 15
General Health Issues: Allergies, Parasites, And Vaccinations

	150
The Role Of Your Veterinarian	150
Allergies	151
Inhalant And Environmental Allergies	153
Contact Allergies	153
Fleas And Ticks	155
Parasitic Worms	157
Heartworms	158
Intestinal Worms: Hookworms, Roundworms, Tapeworms, And Whipworms	159
Vaccinating Your Boston Terrier	161
Holistic Alternatives	163

CHAPTER 16
Genetic Health Concerns Common To The Boston Terrier

	164
Hip And Elbow Dysplasia	164
Hemivertebrae	166
Patellar Luxation	167
Eye Issues	167
Entropion	167
Cherry Eye	167
Corneal Ulcers	167
Glaucoma	169
Keratitis Sicca	169
Injuries	169
Fungal Ear Infections	169
Common Owner Mistakes	170
Prevention And Monitoring	171

CHAPTER 17
The Aging Boston Terrier ... 172
Senior Care Challenges ... 174
    Common Physical Disorders Related To Aging ... 176
    Steps, Ramps, And Wheelchairs ... 176
Vet Visits ... 178
    The Importance Of Regular Vet Visits And What To Expect ... 178
Changes To Watch For ... 179
    Appetite And Nutritional Requirements ... 179
    Exercise ... 179
    Aging And The Senses ... 180
Keeping Your Senior Dog Mentally Active ... 181
Advantages To The Senior Years ... 182
Preparing To Say Goodbye ... 182
Grief And Healing ... 184

INTRODUCTION

The Boston Terrier is an incredibly popular breed whose origins are right there in the name – Boston. While they have less than two centuries as a distinct breed, they have gained their immense popularity because they are such wonderful and charming dogs. They have earned their name as the American Gentleman both because they look like they are wearing a tuxedo and because they are so affable.

The Boston Terrier's personality today is completely different from what it was when they were originally bred. Initially bred to be a pit-fighter back in the 19th century, the Boston Terrier quickly proved that he was not a good fit for the job. That's because, whether you have young children, other dogs, or even cats, the Boston Terrier just wants to be friends with pretty much everyone in his family.

With an intellect that means you can train them to do any number of tricks, you can have a great time playing with your Boston Terrier. Of course, as with any intelligent dog, you are going to have to be careful about what you leave lying around, particularly food. Those cute puppy-dog eyes will make it much harder to put your foot down, and they'll do their best to make you think that you have done enough training for one day. Don't be fooled though. If you give in, they will become even more stubborn the more you let them get away with. You definitely want to make sure that your Boston Terrier is well trained to reduce those bouts of stubbornness and teach your pup to be a bit calmer than his usual hyperactive self.

As you can tell with a quick look, those small bodies are quite sturdy under that black and white fur. Their large eyes look up at you past a short little snout. It is difficult not to fall in love with this breed. The large ears just enhance that sweet look. And their short hair makes them easy to groom.

This is a brachycephalic breed (a dog with a short snout), and that comes with all of the potential health issues to the dog's respiratory system and eyes. They may suffer from overheating because of their short nose and they also have some issues with their large eyes. You are going to need to be prepared for the noise that comes with the breed. Snorting, snoring, and chop licking are going to be constant. The Boston Terrier's compact build also means the breed is quite flatulent. It's a small price to pay for such a loving dog, but it can come as a surprise.

Introduction

The Boston Terrier is a great dog for any sized home and nearly any family. Bringing one into your home is akin to living with a best friend. They aren't aggressive or yappy, and they are much more interested in having fun than in showing who is boss.

CHAPTER 1
An All-American Dog

One look at this cute little dog is enough to steal most people's hearts. Boston Terriers look dapper and have an absolutely charming little personality. They are one of the few dogs from the US that have a name that actually identifies their place of origin, making it quite obvious that they are an American dog.

Their Roots As Fighters

Photo Courtesy of Marianne Bannerman

It is thought that the Boston Terrier was a result of cross breeding the English Bulldog and the white English Terrier, which is now extinct. This explains the variety of coats, all of which look like a very well-dressed dog. The breed was likely a result of the English blood sports that were popular at the time. The breeders wanted a smaller breed of dog that would fight well in a pit. However, the result was not a fierce dog.

The first Boston Terrier was probably bred in the 1860s, and some people think the first one was named Judge. When Judge was sold to William O'Brien, he brought the dog back to Boston, Massachusetts. Judge was slightly bigger than many of his descendants, weighing 32 lbs. He had the brindle colors of the bulldog with a white chest. Half of his face was dark brindle, and the other half white.

Over time, the Boston Terrier was bred to be smaller, but never lost that very compact frame and adorable face. During the early days, they were called Round Head, but by the 1890s, they were renamed to reflect where the breed had become most common.

CHAPTER 1 An All-American Dog

The American Gentleman

With the change of the dog's name to the Boston Terrier came a wealth of interest by locals. In 1891, the Boston Terrier Club of America was founded as a way of promoting the new breed. Just two years later the little charmer had already gained the attention of the American Kennel Club, and was registered that year. While this was a huge step toward getting recognition, Boston Terriers had a long way to go to establish the look and personality for which they are famous today. The breed was still only a couple of decades old at the time, so there was no set standard for their appear-

Photo Courtesy of Lisa Mazurek

Photo Courtesy of Allyson Vokaty

ance. By 1900, the Boston Terrier had become as popular as the pug and toy spaniels among upper-class Americans.

Unlike many other terriers, the Boston Terrier was naturally a very charming breed, less interested in chasing small animals and more interested in being with people. The gentle disposition that made them terrible fighters made them perfect as companions. Over time, the breed got smaller and smaller. There weren't many other comparable small breeds in the US at the time, and this was a breed that really made a great impression. Because of this, people began to call Boston Terriers the American Gentlemen by the turn of the century.

A History Of Companionship

For nearly all of the over 100 years that it has been recognized, the Boston Terrier has been known as a very companionable dog. After all, they largely failed as the fighter they were bred to be because they were just too affable. Breeders wanted to enhance that affable personality, and they were very successful. The Boston Terrier is unique in both its look and its personality.

By the 1920s the breed was the most popular dog in the US. Marketers used them as a way of getting attention from potential customers in their ads. Boston University selected the dog as their mascot.

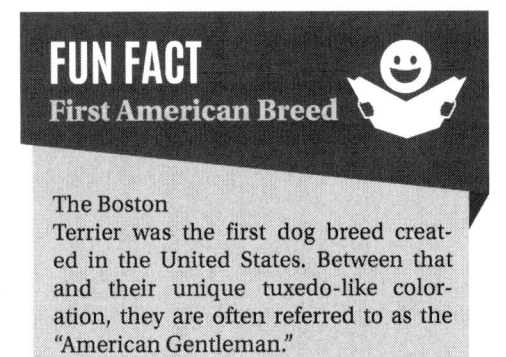

FUN FACT
First American Breed

The Boston Terrier was the first dog breed created in the United States. Between that and their unique tuxedo-like coloration, they are often referred to as the "American Gentleman."

CHAPTER 1 An All-American Dog

Photo Courtesy of Stephanie Hess

When the Great Depression set in, dogs were largely forgotten as people struggled to live. During this time, people bred new dogs because pure breeds were too expensive. This saw a drop in Boston Terrier breeding, but the dogs did not disappear. In 1979, Massachusetts named the breed their state dog.

Although there are new breeds constantly being bred (particularly the doodle types), the Boston Terrier has seen a resurgence in popularity within the United States. You can find them appearing more often in advertising and on shirts and backpacks. They are fantastic play pals, and are increasingly being used to help with pet therapy and as service dogs.

CHAPTER 2
Compact Dog With a Large Personality

The Boston Terrier is a happy-go-lucky dog that loves to be in the middle of the action. Don't be fooled by the small size – the Boston Terrier has a personality that makes it far more similar to larger dogs. Averaging between 10 and 25 lbs., this is a dog that has a lot of muscle on a fairly small frame. With a coat that looks like a tuxedo, this well-dressed gentleman is hard to miss, especially when that boisterous personality comes out.

Photo Courtesy of Lisa Mazurek

CHAPTER 2 Compact Dog With a Large Personality

The Defining Physical Characteristics Of The Boston Terrier

The Boston Terrier does have a distinctive look, but the breed can be confused for the French Bulldog. Both breeds have their roots in the larger English Bulldog, but the high energy is a pretty good indicator that you are interacting with a Boston Terrier and not the more mellow French Bulldog.

Standing at about 1.4 ft tall, Boston Terriers are most easily identified by that compact frame covered with a black and white coat. They may also have brindle in place of the usual black. However, the look is always more like a tux than a consistent pattern across their body. They are slightly taller than the French Bulldog because they have longer legs, and they are less stocky.

Photo Courtesy of Deb Chorzempa

Their brachycephalic face means that they have a short snout, which is further highlighted by their very large eyes. Their head is more like a boxer's. Their large, rounded ears tend to point outward.

Boston Terriers also have short, stumpy tails that usually stick straight out and flare at the end. French Bulldogs tend to have more spiral-like tails that come to a point.

Health Problems Common To Boston Terriers

Boston Terriers have a lot of potential health issues, largely stemming from the fact that they have such short, flat noses. However, they do have some other health concerns that you should know about so that you can monitor your little dog for signs of health problems. With an average life span of between 12 and 14 years, you want to ensure your dog has as long and health a life as possible.

Photo Courtesy of Sonya Johnson

CHAPTER 2   Compact Dog With a Large Personality

Lots Of Genetic Issues

That flat nose can cause respiratory problems, particularly in the heat. They aren't able to cool off as quickly as dogs with longer snouts, so you will need to be careful about taking your Boston Terrier out in hot weather. Because of this tendency to overheat, Boston Terriers are not a breed that should be considered as a jogging companion.

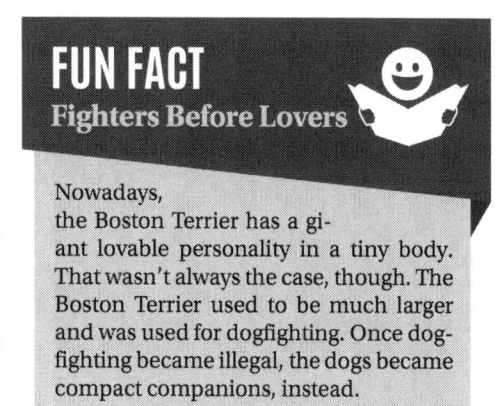

> **FUN FACT**
> **Fighters Before Lovers**
>
> Nowadays, the Boston Terrier has a giant lovable personality in a tiny body. That wasn't always the case, though. The Boston Terrier used to be much larger and was used for dogfighting. Once dogfighting became illegal, the dogs became compact companions, instead.

They also have a number of eye issues, particularly due to irritation and injury. To best protect your dog's eyes, you should make sure to clear your home of things that could scratch your dog's eyes. This includes your yard. When you go out walking, keep your Boston Terrier away from brambles and thickets that could easily hurt him.

They are prone to herniated discs and a number of other back issues, so you always want to be careful about how you play with your Boston Terrier. Always avoid playing rough with him.

You will also need to be careful of degenerative myelopathy, a spinal nerve disorder that begins to show when dogs are five years old or older. It lowers your dog's ability to get around and means he has less control over his bowels. You will notice that your dog will have trouble standing up or walking in the early onset of the disease, as well as a likely increase in accidents in the home. There are ways to help your dog, though there is no known cure.

Like other small dogs, Boston Terriers are also likely to develop luxating patella (a disorder of the kneecaps).

Chapters 3 and 16 provide more details about these diseases, what they are, what breeders do to prevent the genetic disorders, and how to prevent or monitor for them.

A Warning About Allergies And Stomach Sensitivities

This is a breed that has environmental allergies. Check out Chapters 14 and 15 for details.

There is also a potential for your dog to either have a sensitive stomach or food allergies. Chapter 12 provides more details on recommended diets for Boston Terriers to minimize food allergies and sensitivities.

A Charming Entertainer

"Boston's rarely ever meet a stranger. They tend to Love everyone they meet."

Linda Reaves
Bama's Hurricane Creek Kennel

Photo Courtesy of Annette Hostetter Sundberg

Nearly from the moment the first Boston Terrier arrived in the US, the focus was on making the breed a best friend to the family. As a small dog, a Boston Terrier can go pretty much anywhere with you, and he will want to be wherever you are. Boston Terriers do tend to pick a favorite person in the family, and that person will get the majority of the dog's love. However, Boston Terriers will be more than happy to play with the whole family and to let you know when someone is at the door.

They can work well as a watchdog, but with their size and preference for loving instead of fighting, they are not guard dogs. Apart from barking at the door, they are not a breed that tends to be vocal, so you won't have to worry about yapping. Nor are they aggressive, although some males will act a little tough around neighborhood dogs.

While you really can't jog with a Boston Terrier, they do love being active. You can take them on regular walks, hikes, and out to the park. You won't have to worry about your dog being a problem. It is more likely that your Boston Terrier will want to play and charm the people you encounter. However, he will also enjoy just lounging on the couch. Ultimately, your dog is just going to want to hang out with his people.

If you want a dog that is capable of doing tricks, the Boston Terrier is a fantastic choice. That desire for attention and affection coupled with intelligence means your Boston Terrier will be more than happy to learn new tricks. You can also sign him up for a number of different sports, such as agility training.

A Fantastic Dog For An Urban Home

Given their small stature and generally quiet disposition, Boston Terriers are a perfect dog for people who live in apartments. Though they have energy, 20 to 30 minutes of training a day is sufficient. You will need to walk your Boston Terrier a couple of times of day, but you won't need to take long walks to tire your pup. They are playful, so they can entertain you when the weather is too bad to go outside. They know how to entertain or relax, whatever you want to do. They are just happy to be with you.

A Warning About Snorting, Slobbering, And Flatulence

When you have a Boston Terrier what you will learn is that when he is around, you will know it. Since your little friend is pretty much going to stay in the same room as you, you will hear snorting and snoring nearly all of the time. You will have to learn how to sleep with your adult Boston Terrier's heavy snores, particularly when your canine reaches his golden years.

Boston Terriers have a physical build that promotes something that bothers many people: they are incredibly flatulent. After eating or in the morning, they are likely to gas you while you are trying to relax. You can minimize this by giving your dog a natural diet that includes fresh foods instead of commercial food, but preparing the meals can be time consuming. After a while, you will get accustomed to the smell, and it probably won't bother you much at all. It will just be a joke within the family.

For all of this, Boston Terriers are an amazing breed. People who love them see these traits as foibles that make the dogs even more endearing.

CHAPTER 3
Finding Your Boston Terrier

If you have reached this point in the book, you are probably excited about getting your little Boston Terrier. With the big decision about what breed to bring home, you are up to your next big decision – do you want an adult or a puppy? There are pros and cons to both life stages.

Considerations And Steps To Rescue An Adult Boston Terrier

How much work can you manage? Will you be able to deal with an excitable puppy that has everything to learn? Or do you prefer to work with an adult that may have problems that you have to help the dog work through? Puppies are almost always more work, but you never know what kind of experience an adult dog has been through which will affect how he reacts to the world around him.

The hunt to find your newest family member is going to take a while, even if you decide to rescue an adult. There are a number of genetic disorders associated with Boston Terriers, as well as problems that can result from improper breeding and care at the beginning of a Boston Terrier's life. To ensure that you get a healthy puppy that will be your loving companion for as long as possible, you'll need to find a reputable breeder who cares more about the puppies than the money.

The approach to adopting an adult Boston Terrier is the same as it is for adopting a puppy from a breeder. However, with such an intelligent dog, you are going to want to ask a lot more questions about adopting an adult, particularly about the dog's previous experiences.

> **HELPFUL TIP**
> **Rescue**
>
> Since the Boston Terrier is the 21st most popular dog in America, the breed is more commonly found in rescues than less popular dogs. Consider finding your Boston Terrier at a shelter or through a local rescue group rather than buying a puppy from a breeder.

CHAPTER 3 Finding Your Boston Terrier

Photo Courtesy of Jason Pichler

Considerations

Rescuing any dog comes with some inherent risks. While it is possible to find Boston Terrier puppies at dog rescues, it is much more likely that you will find a rescued adult. Adopting an older Boston Terrier could require a lot of work, and their history is incredibly important so you know what to expect. Since the dogs can be stubborn, people may give up on a Boston Terrier without putting much effort into it.

Think about the following to determine if an adult Boston Terrier is a good fit for your home.

- Why do you want to bring an adult into your home? What are your expectations for the dog?
- Boston Terrier are adorable. They may understand the commands you are giving, but they may be particularly stubborn if they haven't been properly trained. Do you have the patience to work through the issues that an adult may have?

Rescue organizations collect as much information as they can about the dogs they rescue, but their knowledge of a dog's history is usually limited. The benefits of rescuing a Boston Terrier are similar to adopting any rescue dog. You need to know about their temperament so you can start planning how to help the dog to overcome past experiences and how to resolve the issues. The odds are very good that you aren't going to be starting from scratch with housetraining. Adult dogs are awake more often than puppies and, while it may take them a bit longer to warm up to you, you can bond much faster with an adult, depending on their age. Adult Boston Terriers may be a bit more wary, especially if they were not socialized or were previously treated poorly, but that loving disposition will likely come out fairly quickly once they start to feel safe and at home. Once your adult dog bonds with you, it will be like flipping an affection switch, and then you really could not ask for a more loving and intelligent canine.

- Are you able to properly dog proof your home before the dog arrives?

You can't simply bring an adult dog into your home and let him run around unchecked. One thing that is similar to preparing your home for puppies is that you will want to dog proof your home for a rescued adult before the dog arrives. Most people think it isn't necessary to prepare for an adult dog and fail to properly get their home ready. Like a puppy, you will

CHAPTER 3   Finding Your Boston Terrier

need to have a dedicated space for your new dog to make sure he learns the rules before being allowed to roam the home. In the beginning you will need a space for the dog to get familiar with you and your home as you assess your new dog's personality and capabilities. It is a fairly important consideration, particularly if you have other dogs and cats, as you will want to ensure harmony in your home.

- Do you have pets who will be affected by a new dog?

Boston Terriers aren't usually much of a problem, but you will want to be careful introducing them in your home. Typically, other dogs will be the problem, but Boston Terriers can be very wary in the beginning, depending on what they've been through before coming to your home.

Good Boston Terrier-specific rescue organizations are cautious about adopting out a rescue with personality and socialization issues. Rescue shelters will be less careful about adopting out Boston Terriers because they are popular and low risk to most homes.

You may not be able to get a complete health record for an adult Boston Terrier, but it is likely that you will find a dog that has already been spayed or neutered, as well as chipped. Unless you adopt a Boston Terrier that has health issues (these should be disclosed by the rescue organization if available), rescues tend to be less costly at the first vet visit than puppies – for the first few years it's likely you won't pay nearly as much to take care of your Boston Terrier's health. You will be spending a lot more time training though. Puppies have a short attention span, which equates to many short training sessions. Adults require more attention and long durations of training so that they get accustomed to listening to you. This dedicated attention is good not only for teaching the rules of the home, but for bonding with the dog.

Older dogs give you more immediate gratification. You don't have to go through those sleepless nights with a new puppy or the endless frustration that comes with the early types of training. All intelligent dogs require a lot of the same time and attention as puppies. Bypassing that is a major part of the appeal of older dogs.

Finally, one of the biggest benefits of getting an adult (besides getting to skip housetraining) – they are already their full size. You don't have to guess the size your adult dog will be, making it far easier to get the right gear and dog supplies in the beginning.

The following are some Boston Terrier rescue organizations to help you get started:

- Boston Terrier Club of America

- American Boston Terrier Rescue & Rehabilitation
- Northeast Boston Terrier Rescue, Inc.
- Midwest Boston Terrier Rescue

Many states have their own dedicated Boston Terrier rescues and clubs. They are a popular breed, so you can find one within your state, or perhaps even in your local area, with a little bit of online research. Start at http://ibostonterrier.com/boston-terrier-rescues to find reputable rescues near you in the US or Canada.

Don't forget that breeders may also have older dogs that they are willing to adopt out to a loving family. Contracts and guarantees are meant as much to protect the puppies as the families who adopt them. If you want an adult, consider calling breeders to see if they have any adults available. You will need to ask them a different set of questions than if you were adopting a puppy, but they will be able to provide you with a lot of details about the dog, his personality, and if there are any potential issues.

Steps To Rescuing A Boston Terrier

If you are interested in looking into adopting from a rescue organization or group, there are several things to keep in mind. This section covers the questions you should ask. If you are considering adopting a puppy from a rescue group instead of a breeder, ask the same questions.

> **To get a better idea of the rescue organization and how much they know about the dogs they adopt out, ask the following questions.**
>
> - What was the reason the dog was surrendered?
> - Did the dog have any health issues when he arrived?
> - Do they know how the dog was treated by the previous family (including what kind of training the dog has had, if he was mistreated, or if he was socialized)?
> - How many homes do they know the dog has been in?
> - What kind of vet care has the dog had? Do they have records from before the dog arrived into their care?
> - Will the dog require extra medical attention based on known or suspected problems?
> - Is the dog housetrained?
> - How well does the dog react to strangers and walks in familiar areas?
> - Does the dog have good eating habits? Does he tend to be more aggressive when eating?
> - How does the dog react to children and other pets?
> - Are there any known allergies?
> - Does the dog have any known additional dietary restrictions?
> - Will the organization take the dog back if there are problems identified with the dog after adoption?

Breeders can be a great source for adopting older Boston Terriers, particularly if you already have pets in the home. Since the adult dog is currently living with other dogs, it means that they have a certain level of socialization. Breeders also have a more complete knowledge of the Boston Terrier's history, which is always preferable for pure breeds.

Considerations For Adopting A Puppy And Picking A Breeder

Puppies are a major time investment, and a dog as intelligent and stubborn as the Boston Terrier will make some aspects of raising a puppy that much harder.

Think about the following to determine if a Boston Terrier puppy is a good fit for your home.

- How much time do you have available? Are you willing to give up all of your free time and work your schedule around your puppy?

One of the biggest considerations is how much time are you willing to invest. All puppies are a lot of work, starting with the moment the puppy enters your care. While the Boston Terrier's temperament is largely predictable, how you train and socialize your puppy will affect nearly every aspect of the dog's adult life. Training and socializing can take up a large chunk of time in the early days, but they are absolutely essential for raising a healthy Boston Terrier.

You also want the puppy to know that your home is safe and that everyone has the puppy's best interest in mind.

- Are you able to be firm and consistent with such an adorable puppy?

CHAPTER 3   Finding Your Boston Terrier

From the very beginning, you have to establish yourself and your family as the ones in charge so that your Boston Terrier understands the hierarchy from the moment he enters your home. All intelligent dogs require additional time to train because they are going to be stubborn. You will need to be prepared to be patient and consistent, no matter how frustrated you are or how cute those puppy eyes are.

- Do you have the time, energy, and budget to puppy proof your home?

The work to prepare your home for your puppy's arrival begins long before your puppy arrives. Puppy proofing the home is as time-consuming as childproofing your home. If you do not have the time to puppy proof your home, then you should consider getting an adult dog. Chapter 5 provides details about what you need to do to prepare your home.

On the plus side, you will have more time with a puppy than with an adult. You will have records about the puppy and the puppy's parents, making it easier to identify the potential problems your Boston Terrier may suffer. This makes it considerably easier to ensure your puppy stays healthy and to catch potential issues earlier.

Some people find it easier to bond with puppies than with adult dogs. A young puppy is going to be nervous in a new home, but most of them adjust quickly because they are predisposed to enjoying the company of those around them. Your primary job will be protecting your puppy and making sure that you patiently train him. We will cover this more in a later chapter.

Finding a responsible breeder is the best thing you can do for your puppy since good breeders work with only healthy parents, reducing the odds that a puppy will have serious health issues. Always take the time to research breeders. Although breeders for Boston Terriers are largely reputable, that doesn't mean there won't be some who are more interested in earning a lot of money than in caring for their dogs.

FUN FACT
Snoring, and Farting, and Drooling, Oh My!

The smushed face of the Boston Terrier leads to snoring and drooling. Bostons are also prone to being gassy. If you can't handle snoring, farting, and drooling, a Boston may not be the breed for you.

Choosing A Breeder

"A good breeder should be able to answer all of your questions on the breed and offer a written health guarantee on the puppy."

Markella Motz
Bly Mountain Bostons

Once you understand enough about the breed to know what you are getting into, it is time to start talking to breeders. The goal is to determine which breeders are willing to take the time to patiently and thoroughly answer all of your questions. They should have as much love for their Boston Terriers as they want you to feel for your new puppy. And they should want to make sure that their puppies go to good homes.

If you find someone who posts regular pictures and information about the parents and the progress of the mother's pregnancy and vet visits, that is a good sign. The best breeders will not only talk about their dogs and the plans for the parents in the future, they will stay in contact with you after you take the puppy home and answer any questions as they arise. These are the kinds of breeders who are likely to have waiting lists. The active interest in knowing about what happens to the puppies later shows that they care a great deal about each individual dog. You also want to find a breeder who is willing to talk about the potential problems with Boston Terriers. Good breeders will want to ensure the family adopting one of their puppies is capable of properly socializing and training a Boston Terrier. Both of these activities are essential as a puppy matures.

It is likely that for each breeder you call the conversation will last about an hour. If a breeder does not have time to talk and isn't willing to talk with you later, you can cross them off your list. After you have talked with each possible breeder, compare answers.

The following are some questions to ask. Make sure you take careful notes while interviewing the breeders:

- Ask if you can visit in person. The answer should always be yes, and if it isn't, you don't need to ask anything further. Thank the breeder and hang up. Even if the breeder is located in a different state, they should allow you to visit the facility.
- Ask about the required health tests and certifications they have for their puppies. These points are detailed further in the next section, so make sure to check off the available tests and certifications for

CHAPTER 3   Finding Your Boston Terrier

each breeder. If they don't have all of the tests and certifications, you may want to remove the breeder from consideration.

- Make sure that the breeder always takes care of all of the initial health requirements in the first few weeks through the early months, particularly shots. Puppies require that certain procedures be done before they leave their mother to ensure they are healthy. Vaccinations and worming typically start around six weeks after the puppies are born, then need to be continued every three weeks. By the time your puppy is old enough to come home, he should be well into the procedures, or even completely through with the first phases of these important health care needs.

- Ask if the puppy is required to be spayed or neutered before reaching a certain age of maturity. Typically, these procedures are done in the puppies' best interest.

- Find out if the breeder is part of a Boston Terrier organization or group.

- Ask about the first phases of your puppy's life, such as how the breeder plans to care for the puppy during those first few months. They should be able to provide a lot of detail, and they should do this without sounding as though they are irritated that you want to know. They will also let you know how much training you can expect to be done prior to the puppy's arrival in your home. It is possible that the breeder may start housetraining the puppy. Ask how quickly the puppy has picked up on the training. You want to be able to pick up from where the breeder left off once your Boston Terrier reaches your home.

- See what kind of advice the breeder gives about raising your Boston Terrier puppy. They should be more than happy to help guide you to doing what is best for your dog because they will want the puppies to live happy, healthy lives. You should also be able to rely on a breeder's recommendations, advice, and additional care after the puppy arrives at your home. Basically, you are getting customer support, as well as a great chance of having a healthy dog.

- How many breeds do they manage a year? How many sets of parents do the breeders have? Puppies can take a lot of time and attention, and the mother should have some downtime between pregnancies. Learn about the breeder's standard operations to find out if they are taking care of the parents and treating them like valuable family members and not strictly as a way to make money.

- Ask about aggression in the parents. Also find out if they have other dog breeds in the home. While puppies are more temperamentally malleable than adults, if they have already had some exposure to other breeds, it may make it easier to integrate them into a home that already has dogs.

Contracts And Guarantees

Breeder contracts and guarantees are meant to protect the puppies as much as they are meant to protect you. If a breeder has a contract that must be signed, make sure that you read through it completely and are willing to meet all of the requirements prior to signing it. The contracts tend to be fairly easy to understand and comply with, but you should be aware of all the facts before you agree to anything. Beyond putting down the money for the puppy, signing the contract says that you are serious about how you plan to take care of the puppy to the best of your abilities by meeting the minimum requirements set forth by the breeder. A contract may also say that the breeder will retain the puppy's original registration papers, although you can get a copy of the papers.

When a family does not live up to the agreement from the contract, the breeder is able to take the puppy from that family. These are the dogs that some breeders have available for adoption.

The guarantee states what health conditions the breeder promises for their puppies. This typically includes details about the dog's health and recommendations on the next steps of the puppy's care once it leaves the breeder's facility. Guarantees may also provide schedules to ensure that the health care started by the breeder is continued by the new puppy parent. In the event that a major health concern is found, the puppy will need to be returned to the breeder. The contract will also explain what is not guaranteed. The guarantee tends to be long (sometimes longer than the contract), and you should read it thoroughly before you sign it.

Boston Terrier contracts usually come with a requirement to have the dog spayed or neutered once it reaches maturity (typically six months). The contract may also contain naming requirements, health details, and a stipulation for what will happen if you can no longer take care of the animal (the dog usually goes back to the breeder). It could also include information on what will happen if you are negligent or abusive to your dog.

Health Tests And Certifications

"At the minimum your new puppies parents should have their Eyes (CAER), Hearing (BAER), Patella, and JHC DNA tests. Your breeder should also offer a health guarantee of some sort."

Lorene Jones
Ta-Koda Boston Terriers

A healthy puppy requires healthy parents and a clean genetic history. A good breeder keeps extensive records of each puppy and the parents. You will want to review each of the parents' complete history to understand what traits your puppy is likely to inherit. Pay attention to learning abilities, temperament, clinginess, and any personality trait you consider important. You can either request that documents be sent electronically to you or get them when you visit the breeder in person.

It could take a while to review the breeder's information about each parent, but it is always well worth the time you spend studying and planning. The more you know about the parents, the better prepared you will be for your puppy.

When looking for a Boston Terrier to adopt, there are several health concerns that you should ask breeders or rescue groups about.

The following are health tests all breeders should ensure their Boston Terriers undergo:

- Patellar luxation
- Hip and elbow evaluation – testing the puppies for dysplasia
- Eye examination by someone who is a member of the ACVO Ophthalmologist (they should be registered with either the OFA or the CERF)
- BAER testing for hearing loss

Breeders who take the time to join the Boston Terrier Club of America prove that they are serious about the health of their puppies. This organization requires that a standardized set of requirements be met, so membership denotes that the breeders who join are reliable and reputable.

Selecting A Puppy From A Breeder

Selecting your puppy should be done in person. However, you can start checking out your puppy after birth if the breeder is willing to share videos and pictures. Once you are allowed to see the puppies in person, consider the following:

- Assess the group of puppies as a whole. If most or all of the puppies are aggressive or fearful, this is an indication of a problem with the litter or (more likely) the breeder. Here are a few red flags if displayed by a majority of the puppies:
  - Tucked tails
  - Shrinking away from people
  - Whimpering when people get close
  - Constant attacking of your hands or feet (beyond pouncing)
- Notice how well each puppy plays with the others. This is a great indicator of just how well your puppy will react to any pets you already have at home.
- Notice which puppies greet you first, and which ones hang back to observe.

CHAPTER 3 Finding Your Boston Terrier

- The puppies should not be fat or underweight. A swollen stomach is generally a sign of worms or other health problems.
- Puppies should have straight, sturdy legs. Splayed legs can be a sign that there is something wrong.
- Examine the puppy's ears for mites, which will cause discharge. The inside of the ear should be pink, not red or inflamed.
- The eyes should be clear and bright.
- Check the puppy's mouth for pink, healthy-looking gums.
  - Pet the puppy to check his coat for the following:
    - Ensure that the coat feels thick and full. If the breeder has allowed the fur to get matted or really dirty, it is an indication that they likely are not taking proper care of the animals.
    - Check for fleas and mites by running your hand from the head to the tail, then under the tail (fleas are more likely to hide under most dogs' tails). Mites may look like dandruff.
- Check the puppy's rump for redness and sores and see if you can check the last bowel movement to ensure it is firm.

Pick the puppy that exhibits the personality traits that you want in your dog. If you want an outgoing, friendly, excitable dog, the first puppy to greet you may be the one you seek. If you want a dog that will think things through and let others get more attention, look for a puppy that sits back and observes you before approaching.

CHAPTER 4
Preparing Your Family

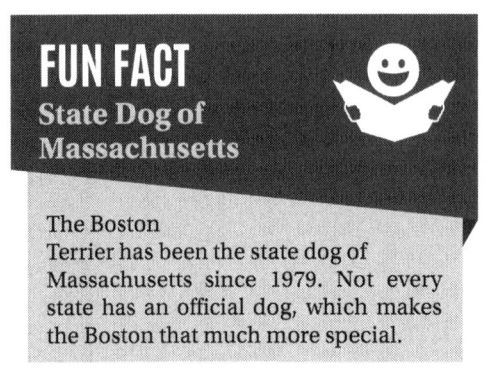

FUN FACT
State Dog of Massachusetts

The Boston Terrier has been the state dog of Massachusetts since 1979. Not every state has an official dog, which makes the Boston that much more special.

As excited as your family may be about the arrival of a new family member, there are a good number of tasks that need to be done before your new dog arrives. You need to determine who will be responsible for the different needs of the dog, as well as determining where your new dog will be for at least the first couple of weeks (even an adult dog will need to have dedicated space in the beginning as you get to know each other). You will need to establish who is the primary person responsible, and make sure all of the members of your family keep this in mind. That is just one of the first rules that you must make sure is in place before your Boston Terrier arrives.

Planning The First Year's Budget

Caring for a puppy is a lot more expensive than you might think. You will need to have a budget, which is a good reason to start purchasing supplies a few months in advance. When you buy the items you need, you will begin to see exactly how much you will spend a month. Of course there are some items that are one-time purchases, but many other items will need to be purchased regularly, like food and treats.

Begin budgeting the day you decide to get your puppy. The cost will include the adoption fee, which is typically higher for a purebred dog than for a rescue dog.

The vet and other healthcare costs, such as regular vaccinations and an annual checkup, should be included in your budget.

The following table can help you start to plan your budget. Keep in mind that the prices are a rough averages, and may be significantly different based on where you live.

Item	Considerations	Estimated Costs
Crate	This should be a comfortable space where the puppy will sleep and rest.	Wire crates: Range $60 to $350 Portable crate: Range $35 to $200
Bed	This will be placed in the crate.	$10 to $55
Leash	It should be short in the beginning because you need to be able to keep your puppy from getting overexcited and running to the end of a long line.	Short leash: $6 to $15 Retractable: $8 to $25
Doggie bags for walks	If you walk at parks, this won't be necessary. For those who don't have daily access to bags, it is best to purchase packs to ensure you don't run out of bags.	Singles cost less than $1 each. Packs: $4 to $16
Collar	This should fit comfortably without being too loose or tight. It can be difficult to get it right at first, and you will need to adjust it as your puppy grows.	$10 to $30
Tags	These will likely be provided by your vet. Find out what information the vet provides on tags, then purchase any tags that are not provided. At a minimum, your Boston Terrier should have tags with your address on it in case the pup escapes.	Contact your vet before purchasing to see if the required rabies tags include your contact info.
Puppy food	This will depend on if you make your Boston Terrier food, if you purchase food, or both. The larger the bag, the higher the cost, but the fewer times you will need to purchase food. You will need to purchase puppy specific food in the beginning, but will stop after the second year. Adult dog food is more expensive, so you will need to plan for an increase in cost once your puppy reaches adulthood.	$9 to $90 per bag

Water and food bowls	These will need to be kept in the puppy's designated area. If you have other dogs, you will need separate food bowls for the puppy. If your puppy proves to be an avid chewer, consider getting a stainless steel bowl.	$10 to $40
Toothbrush/ Toothpaste	You will need to brush his teeth regularly, so plan to buy more than one toothbrush during the first year.	$2.50 to $14
Brush	Boston Terrier coats are fairly easy to maintain, but you should still brush them regularly. When they are puppies, brushing offers a great way to bond.	$3.50 to $20
Toys	You definitely want to get your puppy toys, and you are going to want toys for more aggressive chewers, even if your puppy goes through them remarkably quickly. You may want to keep getting your Boston Terrier toys as an adult (cost of adult dog toys not included).	$2.00 Packs of toys range from $10 to $20 (easier in the long run as your pup will chew through toys quickly)
Training treats	You will need these from the beginning, and likely won't need to change the treats based on your Boston Terrier's age; you may need to change treats to keep your dog's interest though.	$4.50 to $15

The difference between the puppy and an adult in size is not substantial, so you won't need to get two different crates or other supplies. However, you will need to adjust some of the pet supplies, such as the collar.

CHAPTER 4 Preparing Your Family

Instructing Children

"Be sure any children in the home know how to treat a puppy kind and respectfully and keep their toys off the floor."

Maxine Uzoff
Oui Bostons

You want your pup to feel comfortable from the start, which means making sure your children are careful and gentle with the dog, whether you're planning on adopting a puppy or an adult. This is a breed that looks absolutely adorable, and some kids may try to treat the dog like a toy or stuffed animal, which could be detrimental to your Boston Terrier – especially if you get a puppy. You will need to make sure your kids follow all of the rules from the beginning to ensure that your puppy feels safe and happy in your home.

Photo Courtesy of Jason Pichler

Remind your kids of the following rules regularly, both before the puppy arrives and after. Older teens will probably be all right to help with the puppy, but younger teens and kids should not be left alone with the puppy for a few months. Remember that you will need to be very firm to make sure that the puppy is not hurt or frightened.

The following are the five golden rules that your children should follow from the very first interaction.

1. Always be gentle and respectful.
2. Do not disturb the puppy during mealtime.
3. Chase is an outside game.
4. The Boston Terrier should always remain firmly on the ground. Never pick him up.
5. All of your valuables should be kept well out of the puppy's reach.

CHAPTER 4 Preparing Your Family

Since your kids are going to ask why, here are the explanations you can give them. You can simplify them for younger kids, or start a dialogue with teens.

Always Be Gentle And Respectful

Little Boston Terrier puppies are cute and cuddly, but they are also more fragile than their rugged appearance suggests. At no time should anyone play rough with the puppy (or any adult Boston Terrier). It is important to be respectful of your puppy to help the dog learn to also be respectful toward people and other animals.

This rule must be applied consistently every time your children play with the puppy. Be firm if you see your children getting too excited or rough. You don't want the puppy to get overly excited either because he might end up nipping or biting someone. If he does, it isn't his fault because he hasn't learned better yet – it is the child's fault. Make sure your children understand the possible repercussions if they get too rough.

Mealtime

Boston Terriers, like nearly every breed, can be protective of their food, especially if you rescue a dog that has previously had to fend for himself. Even if you have a puppy, you don't want him to feel insecure about his food because that will teach him to be aggressive when he is eating, which is obviously not fair to your Boston Terrier. Save yourself, your family, and your Boston Terrier trouble by making sure everyone knows that eating time is your Boston Terrier's time alone. Similarly, teach your kids that their own mealtime is off limits to the puppy. No feeding him from the table.

Chase

Make sure your kids understand why a game of chase is fine outside (though you'll need to monitor it), but inside the house the game is off limits.

Running inside the home gives your Boston Terrier puppy the impression that your home isn't safe inside because he is being chased. And it teaches your puppy that running indoors is fine, which can be dangerous as the dog gets older and bigger. One of the last things you want is for your Boston Terrier to go barreling through your home knocking into people because it was fine for him to run in the house when he was a puppy.

Paws On The Ground

This is a rule that will likely require a good bit of explaining to your children as Boston Terriers look a lot like toys, especially Boston Terrier puppies. No one should be picking the puppy up off the ground. You may want to carry your new family member around or play with the pup like a baby, but you and your family will need to resist that urge. Kids particularly have trouble understanding since they will see the Boston Terrier puppy more like a toy than a living creature. The younger your children are, the more difficult it will be for them to understand the difference. It is so tempting to treat the Boston Terrier like a baby and to try to carry him like one, but this is incredibly uncomfortable and unhealthy for the puppy. Older kids will quickly learn that a puppy's nip or bite hurts a lot more than you would think. Those little teeth are quite sharp, and you don't want the puppy to be dropped. If your children learn never to pick up the puppy things will go a lot better. Remember, this also applies to you, so don't make things difficult by doing something you constantly tell your children not to do.

Keep Valuables Out Of Reach

Valuables are not something you want to end up in the puppy's mouth, whether it's toys, jewelry, or shoes. Your kids will be less than happy if their personal possessions are chewed up by an inquisitive puppy, so teach them to put toys, clothes, and other valuables far out of the puppy's reach.

CHAPTER 4 Preparing Your Family

Preparing Your Current Dogs

Boston Terriers tend to be easygoing, so the interaction with your dogs is going to depend on your current dogs' personality. This means if you already have canines in your home, they are going to need to be prepared for the new arrival.

> **Here are the important tasks to do to prepare your current pets for your new arrival.**
> - Set a schedule for activities and the people who will need to participate.
> - Preserve your current dogs' favorite places and furniture, and make sure their toys and items are not in the puppy's space.
> - Have playdates at your home and analyze your dogs to see how they react to an addition.

Stick To A Schedule

Obviously, the puppy is going to get a lot of attention, so you need to make a concerted effort to let your current canine know that you still love and care for him. Make a specific time in your schedule just for your current dog or dogs, and make sure that you don't stray from that schedule after the puppy's arrival.

Make sure that you plan to have at least one adult around for each dog you have. Cats are generally less of a concern, but you will probably want to have at least one other

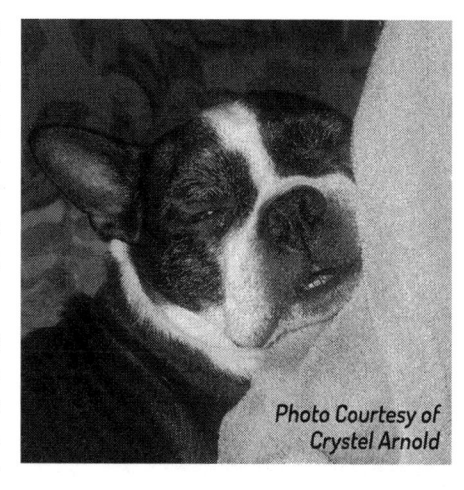

Photo Courtesy of Crystel Arnold

adult around when the puppy comes home. We will go into more detail later about what the roles of the other adults will be, but for now, when you know what date you will be bringing your puppy home, ensure that you have additional adults to help out. You may need to remind them as the time nears, so set an alert on your phone, as well as the date, time, and pick-up information for your puppy.

One benefit of having a schedule for your other dogs in place before your Boston Terrier puppy arrives is that it will then be easy to keep a schedule with the puppy. Boston Terriers love to know what to expect, at least in the beginning.

Your puppy is going to eat, sleep, and spend most of the day and night in his assigned space. This means that the space cannot block your current canine from his favorite furniture, bed, or any place where he rests over the course of the day. None of your current dog's stuff should be in this area, and this includes toys. You don't want your dog to feel like the puppy is taking over his territory. Make sure your children understand to never put your current dog's stuff in the puppy's area.

Your dog and the puppy will need to be kept apart in the early days, (even if they seem friendly) until your puppy is done with vaccinations. Puppies are more susceptible to illness during these days, so wait until the puppy is protected before the dogs spend time together. Leaving the puppy in the puppy space will keep them separated during this critical time.

Helping Your Dog Prepare – Extra At Home Playdates

Here are things that will best help prepare your pooch for the arrival of your puppy.

- Think about your dog's personality to help you decide the best way to prepare for that first day, week, and month. Each dog is unique, so you will need to consider your dog's personality to determine how things will go when the new dog arrives. If your current dog loves other dogs, this will probably hold true when the puppy shows up. If your dog has any territorial tendencies, you will need to be cautious about the introduction and first couple of months so that your current dog learns that the Boston Terrier is now a part of the pack. Excitable dogs will need special attention to keep them from getting overly agitated when a new dog comes home. You don't want them to be so excited they accidentally hurt the little Boston Terrier.

- Consider the times when you have had other dogs in your home and how your current dog reacted to these other furry visitors. If your canine displayed territorial tendencies, you should be extra careful with how you introduce your new pup. If you haven't ever invited another dog to your home, have a couple of playdates with other dogs at your home before your new Boston Terrier puppy arrives. You have to know how your current furry babies will react to new dogs in the house so you can properly prepare. Meeting a dog at home is very different from encountering one outside the home.

- Think about your dog's interactions with other dogs for as long as you have known the pup. Has your dog shown either protective or possessive behavior, either with you or others? Food is one of the reasons dogs will display some kind of aggression because they don't want anyone trying to eat what is theirs. Some dogs can be protective of people and toys too.

The same rules apply, no matter how many dogs you have. Think about the personalities of all of them as individuals, as well as how they interact together. Just like people, you may find that when they are together your dogs act differently, which you will need to keep in mind as you plan their first introduction.

See Chapter 8 for planning to introduce your current dogs and your new puppy, and how to juggle a new puppy and your current pets.

A Friend To Your Whole Family, Even Cats

One of the reasons that so many people are so willing to bring a Boston Terrier into the home is that the breed seems to be perfectly loving and affectionate with everyone. They can be easy to introduce to dogs and cats already in your home. It is more likely that your cats will be annoyed with this new interloper than your Boston Terrier will be interested in chasing the cat. Of course, if your cat runs, the pup is going to think it is a game, but for most Boston Terriers, they just want to play.

CHAPTER 5
Preparing Your Home And Schedule

Whether you bring home a puppy or an adult dog, you are going to need to set up time to prepare your home well in advance of your new Boston Terrier's arrival.

Boston Terriers are adorable little versions of what they will be. Their fur is a bit softer, but the color already shows you exactly what your pup will look like when you get the little fella home. As cute as they are, you have to remember that Boston Terriers are smart dogs, and they are going to be pretty small when they get to your home. That means that they are going to be looking around seeing just what they can explore. This is dangerous for both your puppy and your home. Your Boston Terrier is going to be curious and will try to get into cabinets, low trash cans, and other items around your home that are easily accessible. Preparing your home for a puppy small enough to get into tight spaces is definitely tricky. This means you must take the time to prepare your home before the puppy's arrival.

The week before your puppy arrives, you should conduct numerous checks to ensure that your home is safe for the new family member. Making sure your new Boston Terrier has a safe space with all of the essentials (including toys) will make the arrival of your newest family addition a great time for everyone – especially your new canine companion.

Even if you bring an adult Boston Terrier home, you have to prepare for the arrival of an incredibly headstrong toddler that can get into places that you had not considered remotely possible. Boston Terriers have to learn that you are in control, which means that you have to gain their respect before they will listen to you. This could be challenging if they have not been trained. Like all intelligent breeds, they can be stubborn, refusing to listen until you prove that you are in command If your dog has not already learned not to grab food, climb on furniture, or whatever other restrictions you have implemented in your home, you will have your work cut out for you when it comes to training your new friend. These are all things that you need to be aware your dog could do because adults are much more capable than puppies. Dog-proofing your home will help you keep your dog safe while he is learning to listen to you.

CHAPTER 5 Preparing Your Home And Schedule

Creating A Safe Space For Your Dog Or Puppy

"Get a baby gate and block off a safe area for your puppy to play in. Usually a bathroom, utility room, or kitchen are good areas, especially if it can be easily cleaned and mopped."

*****Linda Reaves*****
Bama's Hurricane Creek Kennel

Your puppy is going to need a dedicated space that includes a crate (more information on this in the next section), food and water bowls, pee pads, and toys. All of these things will need to be in the area where the puppy will be when you are not able to give him attention. The puppy space should be safe and gated so that the puppy cannot get out, and young children and other dogs cannot get in. It should be a safe space where the puppy can see you going about your usual business and feel comfortable.

Photo Courtesy of Corrine Williams

CHAPTER 5   Preparing Your Home And Schedule

Getting The Right Crate

Getting the right crate is important because you want your Boston Terrier to feel comfortable and safe. That means taking the time to prepare something that will be comfortable for crate training. Crate training a Boston Terrier puppy can be fairly easy (much easier than house training), but not if you have a crate that is too big, too small, or too hard for your dog to feel like it is a safe place. To make training easy later, you need to make sure that the puppy's crate and bedding is already set up and ready before your puppy arrives.

Never treat the crate like it is a prison for your puppy. Your Boston Terrier should never associate the crate with punishment – it's meant to be a safe haven after overstimulation or when it's time to sleep. Ensure your dog never associates the crate with punishment or negative emotions. The crate should be adjustable so that you can make it a bit larger when your puppy becomes an adult. You can also get your puppy a carrying crate in the early days to make trips to the vet a little easier. This crate won't work when your Boston Terrier is an adult (you can just walk your dog into the vet's office as an adult), but the carrying crate has plenty of space for a puppy.

You can use the crate to help with housetraining. While Boston terriers tend to be easy to housetrain, you may want to have a pee pad in the puppy's area as far from the crate as possible. This will give your puppy a place to go during inclement weather. Make sure to find out from the breeder if the puppy has already begun housetraining. If the puppy is already making progress, you may not want to add the pee pad.

Purchase And Prepare Supplies And Tools

Planning for your puppy's arrival means buying a lot supplies up front. The list is longer than most people realize, so take some time to really think about what you will need based on your home and circumstances. If you start making purchases around the time you identify the breeder you will get the puppy from, you can stretch out your expenses over a longer period of time. This will make it seem a lot less expensive than it actually is. The following are recommended items you should have purchased before bringing your new dog home:

- Crate
- Bed
- Leash
- Doggie bags for walks
- Collar
- Tags

- Puppy food
- Water and food bowls (sharing a water bowl is usually okay, but your puppy needs his or her own food dish if you have multiple dogs)
- Toothbrush/Toothpaste
- Brush
- Toys
- Training treats

Talk to your vet before buying any medications, including flea treatments.

Puppy Proof The House

> **FUN FACT**
> **The Boston NOT Terrier?**
> Despite the breed name, the American Kennel Club does not classify the Boston as a Terrier. Instead, the breed calls the Non-Sporting Group home.

Preparing for the arrival of a puppy is time consuming, and all of the most dangerous rooms and items in your home will be equally as dangerous to your puppy as they would be to a baby. The biggest difference is that your Boston Terrier is going to be mobile much faster than a child. He will potentially get into dangerous situations almost immediately if you don't eliminate all of the dangers ahead of his arrival in your home.

Be aware that puppies will try to eat virtually anything, even if it isn't food. Nothing is safe – not even your furniture. They'll gnaw on wood and metal. Anything within their reach is considered to be fair game. Keep this in mind as you go about puppy proofing your home.

Indoor Hazards And Fixes

This section details the areas inside your home where you should focus your attention. In case of problems, have your vet's number posted on the fridge and in at least one other room in the house. If you set this up before your pup arrives, it will be there if you need it. Even if you program the vet's phone number into your phone, another family member or someone taking care of your Boston Terrier may still need it.

Boston Terriers can get into nearly everything at their height, and they will be exploring a lot when given the opportunity. As intelligent as the breed is, it's best to overestimate what your puppy can do and prepare accordingly. Get low and see each room from your Boston Terrier's perspective. You are almost guaranteed to find at least one thing you missed.

CHAPTER 5   Preparing Your Home And Schedule

Hazards	Fixes	Time Estimate
Kitchen		
Poisons	Keep in secured, childproof cabinets or on high shelves	30 min
Trash cans	Have a lockable trash can, or keep it in a secured location	10 min
Appliances	Make sure all cords are out of reach	15 min
Human Food	Keep out of reach	Constant (start making it a habit)
Floors		
Slippery surfaces	Put down rugs or special mats designed to stick to the floor	30 min – 1 hour
Training area	Train on non-slip surfaces	Constant
Bathrooms		
Toilet brush	Either have one that locks or keep out of reach	5 min/bathroom
Poisons	Keep in secured, childproof cabinets or on high shelves	15 - 30 min/ bathroom
Toilets	Keep closed. Do _not_ use automatic toilet cleaning chemicals	Constant (start making it a habit)
Cabinets	Keep locked with childproof locks	15 - 30 min/ bathroom
Laundry Room		
Clothing	Store clean and dirty clothing off the floor, and out of reach	15 – 30 min
Poisons (bleach, pods/detergent, dryer sheets, and misc. poisons)	Keep in secured, child-proofed cabinets or on high shelves	15 min
Around the Home		
Plants	Keep off the floor	45 min – 1 hour

Trash cans	Have a lockable trash can, or keep it in a secured location	30 min
Electrical cords, window blind cords	Hide them or make sure they are out of reach; pay particular attention to entertainment and computer areas	1.5 hours
Poisons	Check to make sure there aren't any (WD40, window/screen cleaner, carpet cleaner, air fresheners); move all poisons to a centralized, locked location	1 hour
Windows	Check that cords are out of reach in all rooms	1 – 2 hours
Fireplaces	Store cleaning supplies and tools where the puppy can't get into them Cover the fireplace opening with something the puppy can't knock over	10 min/fireplace
Stairs	Cordon off so that your puppy can't try to go up or down them; make sure to test any puppy gates	10 – 15 min
Coffee tables/End tables/ Nightstands	Clear of dangerous objects (e.g., scissors, sewing equipment, pens, and pencils) and all valuables	30 – 45 min

    If you have a cat, keep the litter box up off the floor. It needs to be somewhere that your cat can easily get to but your Boston Terrier cannot. Since this involves teaching your cat to use the new area, it's something you should do well in advance of the puppy's arrival. You don't want your cat to undergo too many significant changes all at once. The puppy will be enough of a disruption – if your cat associates the change with the puppy, you may find the feline protesting by refusing to use the litter box.

CHAPTER 5 Preparing Your Home And Schedule

Outdoor Hazards And Fixes

This section details the things outside your home that need your attention ahead of your puppy's arrival. Also post the vet's number in one of the sheltered areas in case of an emergency.

Hazards	Fixes	Time Estimate
Garage		
Poisons	Keep in secured, child-proofed cabinets or on high shelves (e.g., car chemicals, cleaning supplies, paint, lawn care) – this includes fertilizer	1 hour
Trash bins	Keep them in a secured location	5 min
Tools (e.g., lawn, car, hardware, power tools)	Make sure all cords are out of reach: Keep out of reach and never hanging over the side of surfaces	30 min – 1 hour
Equipment (e.g., sports, fishing)	Keep out of reach and never hanging over the side of surfaces	Constant (start making it a habit)
Sharp implements	Keep out of reach and never hanging over the side of surfaces	30 min
Bikes	Store off the ground or in a place the Boston Terrier cannot get to (to keep the pup from biting the tires)	20 min
Fencing (Can Be Done Concurrently)		
Breaks	Fix any breaks in the fencing. Boston Terriers are escape artists, so you need to make sure they can't easily get out of your yard.	30 min - 1 hour

Gaps	Fill any gaps, even if they are intentional, so your Boston Terrier doesn't escape	30 min - 1 hour
Holes/Dips at Base	Fill any area that can be easily crawled under	1 – 2 hours
Yard		
Poisons	Don't leave any poisons in the yard	1 – 2 hours
Plants	Verify that all <u>low plants</u> aren't poisonous to dogs; fence off anything that is (such as grape vines)	45 min – 1 hour
Tools (e.g., lawn maintenance and gardening tools)	Make sure they are out of reach; Make sure nothing is hanging over the sides of outdoor tables	30 min - 1 hour

Never leave your Boston Terrier alone in the garage, even when he is an adult. It is likely that your puppy will be in the garage when you take car trips, which is why it is important to puppy proof it.

Boston Terriers are escape artists, and they will come up with many new and inventive ways to get out. Do not make it easy for them; take care of all breaks, gaps, and damage to the fence so that your dog can't make any opening big enough to get out of your yard.

Just like with the inside, you will need to follow up your outdoor preparations by getting low and checking out all areas from a puppy's perspective. Again, you are all but guaranteed to find at least one thing you missed.

HELPFUL TIP
Exercise Needs

You may think that Boston Terriers don't need much exercise because they're so small. Actually, Bostons have tons of energy! Since they're small, you can burn off much of that energy playing inside. However, don't assume a Boston will be the perfect little lapdog with no exercise.

CHAPTER 5 Preparing Your Home And Schedule

Photo Courtesy of Jason Pichler

Choosing Your Veterinarian

Photo Courtesy of Stephanie Hess

Start looking around for a vet for your Boston Terrier even before you choose a breeder. You should have your vet chosen before you bring your dog home. Whether you get a puppy or an adult, you should take your canine to the vet within 48 hours (24 hours is strongly recommended) of his arrival to make sure your dog is healthy. If there is a vet near you who specializes in or has worked with several Boston Terriers before, that will be best for your pup. Considering the Boston Terrier's personality, you want a vet who knows how to work with a headstrong pooch. Getting an appointment with a vet can take a while, especially one that specializes in a particular breed, just like getting a doctor's appointment. You need to have your vet and the first appointment booked well in advance of your dog's arrival.

Here are some things to consider when looking for a vet:

- What is the level of familiarity with Boston Terriers?

    The vet doesn't have to be a specialist, as this is a popular breed. You want your vet to have some experience with them, particularly as the breed has a number of health concerns. Familiarity with the possible problems will help to identify symptoms or potential issues as early as possible.

- How far from your home is the vet?

    You don't want the vet to be more than 30 minutes away in case of an emergency.

- Is the vet available for emergencies after hours or can they recommend a vet in case of an emergency?

- Is the vet part of a local vet hospital if needed, or does the doctor refer patients to a local pet hospital?

CHAPTER 5 Preparing Your Home And Schedule

- Is the vet the only vet or one of several partners? If he or she is part of a partnership, can you stick with just one vet for office visits?
- How are appointments booked?
- Can you have other services performed there, such as grooming and boarding?
- Is the vet accredited?
- What are the prices for the initial visit and the normal costs, such as for shots and regular visits?
- What tests and checks are performed during the initial visit?

Make time to visit the vet you are considering so that you can look around to see what the environment is like inside the office. See if you can speak to the vet to see if he or she is willing to help put you at ease and answer your questions. A vet's time is valuable, but he or she should have a few minutes to help you feel confident that he/she is the right choice to help take care of your canine.

CHAPTER 6
Bringing Your Boston Terrier Home

Bringing home your Boston Terrier is going to be something that you remember for a very long time. You never know exactly how your puppy or adult dog will react, but you know there is going to be just as much uncertainly on his part. With their affable personality and curiosity, you probably aren't going to have nearly so much anxiety as with other small breeds. That curiosity is probably going to win out and your puppy will want to explore. Still, you are going to have to make sure that the exploration is done in a safe environment – no running loose around the home, not even if you bring home an adult. Do expect the adult pup to be a little more wary though as you may not know what his previous experiences were.

Make sure to read Chapter 7 about how to introduce your adult dog to a multi-pet home. While Boston Terriers don't tend to be aggressive, your new dog may not have had a positive experience with other dogs in the past. You want to make sure to take it slow in the early days.

Photo Courtesy of
Kelly Reardon
White Valley Boston Terriers

CHAPTER 6 Bringing Your Boston Terrier Home

Final Preparations And Planning

Most intelligent breeds require a constant presence for the first week and as much of the first month as possible. They can figure out a way of escaping from their enclosure, so you need someone home to stop any escape attempts. You should plan to take time off from work or negotiate working from home during at least the first 24 hours, if not the first 48 hours. The best-case scenario would have you home for the first week or two. The more time you can dedicate to helping your new friend become accustomed to the new surroundings in those first few days, the better for your new family member and the more quickly he will feel comfortable in his new environment.

The following are some useful checklists to get you through the preparation for your puppy and the aftermath of his arrival at your home.

Ensure You Have Food And Other Supplies On Hand

Do a quick check to ensure that you have everything you need. If you created a list based on the basic supplies from Chapter 5, review the list the day before your Boston Terrier arrives and make sure you have everything on it. Take a few moments to consider if there is anything you are missing, too. This will hopefully save you from having to try to rush out to buy additional supplies after the arrival of your new family member.

Design A Tentative Puppy Schedule

Prepare a tentative schedule to help you get started over the course of the week. Your days are about to get very busy, so you need somewhere to start before your puppy arrives. Use the information from Stick to a Schedule to get started, but make sure you do this earlier instead of later. The following are the three important areas to have established for your puppy's schedule:

- Feeding
- Training (including housetraining)
- Playing

When you bring home a puppy, you may be expecting the high energy that you will see when your Boston Terrier is an adult. However, puppies of any breed (no matter how active they will be later) require a lot of sleep. Expect your puppy to sleep between 18 and 20 hours per day. Having a predictable sleep schedule will help your puppy to grow up healthier.

In the beginning, your Boston Terrier won't be high energy, so you won't need to worry about making sure that he is tired out by the end of the day. His stamina will build fairly quickly, though, so by the end of the first year, your pup will be a lot more active. One of the best things about the breed is that they tend to have energy levels appropriate to their situation, so you aren't going to be as hard pressed to tire your Boston Terrier out as you would a Beagle or Jack Russell Terrier. You will still need to make sure that he gets enough exercise based on his caloric intake, but beyond that, your Boston Terrier will probably adopt an energy level that matches your lifestyle.

In the early days, your puppy's schedule will largely revolve around sleeping and eating, with some walking and socialization. Waking hours will include training and play.

Do A Quick Final Puppy Proofing Inspection Before The Puppy Arrives

No matter how busy you are, or how carefully you followed the puppy proofing checklists from the previous chapter, you still need to take the time to inspect your home one more time before the puppy arrives. Set aside an hour or two to complete this a day or two before the puppy arrives.

Initial Meeting

Have a meeting with all of the family members to make sure all of the rules discussed in Chapter 4 are remembered and understood before the puppy is a distraction. This includes how to handle the puppy. Determine who is going to be responsible for primary puppy care, including who will be the primary trainer. To help teach younger children about responsibility, a parent can pair with a child to manage the puppy's care. The child will be responsible for things like keeping the water bowl filled and feeding the puppy, while a parent oversees the tasks.

Picking Up Your Puppy Or Dog And The Ride Home

Picking up your puppy takes a good bit of planning and preparation, especially if you are going to the breeder's home. If possible, plan to pick up your puppy on a weekend or at the beginning of a holiday so you can spend unrushed time at home with him. This section covers the preparation and actual trip, but not what to do if you have other dogs that you need to introduce (Chapter 8).

CHAPTER 6 Bringing Your Boston Terrier Home

As tempting as it is to cuddle with your puppy and try to make the ride home comfortable, using a crate for the ride home is both safer and more comfortable for the puppy. Two adults should be present on the first trip.

- The crate should be anchored in the car for safety and include a cushion inside the crate. If you have a long trip, bring food and water and plan to stop to give them to the puppy on the trip. Do not put them in the crate as they will not be anchored down, and sloshing water can scare your puppy. You can cover the bottom of the crate with a towel or pee pad in case of accidents.

Photo Courtesy of Autumn Narducci

- Call the breeder to make sure everything is still on schedule and make sure the puppy is ready.
- Ask, if you haven't already, if you can get the mother to leave her scent on a blanket to help make the puppy's transition more comfortable.
- Make sure your other adult remembers and will be on time to head to the pick-up destination.
- If you have other dogs, make sure that all of the adults involved know what to do, the time and where to go for that first neutral meeting.

If you do not have other dogs, you can pick up your puppy and head straight home. Do not stop anywhere after you have the puppy. If you have a long trip (more than a couple of hours), build breaks into it every few hours to give your puppy a chance to stretch, exercise, drink, and use the bathroom. Do not leave the puppy alone in the car for any amount of time. If you have to use the restroom, at least one adult must remain with the puppy during each stop.

Ask the breeder if the puppy has been in a car before, and, if not, it is especially important to have someone who can give the puppy attention while the other person drives. The puppy will be in the crate, but someone can still provide comfort. It will definitely be scary because the puppy no longer has mom, siblings, or known people around, so having someone present to talk to the puppy will make it less of an ordeal for the little guy.

This is the time to start teaching your puppy that car trips are enjoyable. This means making sure that the crate is secure. You don't want to terrify the puppy by letting the crate slide around while he is sitting helpless inside it.

FUN FACT
Favored by Helen Keller

Classmates at Radcliffe College gave Helen Keller a Boston Terrier. Although the dog (named Sir Thomas) wasn't a fan of strangers, he and Keller hit it off immediately.

When you arrive home, immediately take the puppy or dog outside to use the bathroom. Even if the puppy or dog had an accident on the way, this is the time to start training your new family member where to use the bathroom.

CHAPTER 6 Bringing Your Boston Terrier Home

Photo Courtesy of Berny Vraa

The First Vet Visit And What To Expect

A vet's visit is necessary within the first day or two of your puppy's arrival and may be required in the contract you signed with the breeder. You need to establish a baseline for the puppy's health so that the vet can track your puppy's progress and monitor to ensure everything is going well as your Boston Terrier grows. The initial assessment gives you more information about your puppy, as well as giving you a chance to ask the vet questions and get advice. It also creates an important rapport between your Boston Terrier and the vet.

That first vet visit will be interesting and different from subsequent visits. Your pup won't know what to expect since he hasn't been to that particular vet before. Try as best as you can to ease his anxiety. You want this first visit to set a positive tone for all future visits.

There are several things that you will need to do before the day of the appointment:

- Find out how early you need to arrive to complete the paperwork for the new patient.
- Find out if you should bring a stool sample for that first visit, too. If so, collect it the morning of the visit and make sure to take it with you.
- Bring in the paperwork provided by the breeder or rescue organization for the vet to add to your pup's or dog's records.

Upon your arrival, your puppy may want to meet the other pups and people in the office, which is something that can be encouraged as long as you keep some basic rules in mind. After all, this is a chance for you to work on socializing the puppy and to create an initial positive experience to associate with the vet, although you will need to be careful. Always ask the owner if it is all right for your puppy to meet any other pet, and wait for approval before letting your puppy move forward with meeting other animals. Pets at the vet's office are likely to not be feeling great, which means they may not be very affable. You don't want a grumpy older dog or a sick animal to nip or scare your puppy. Negative social experiences are something your puppy will remember, and will make going to the vet something to dread or resist. Nor do you want your puppy to be exposed to potential illnesses while still getting his shots.

During the first visit, the vet will conduct an initial assessment of your Boston Terrier. One of the most important things the vet will do is take your puppy's weight. This is something you are going to have to monitor for your Boston Terrier's entire life because the breed is prone to obesi-

CHAPTER 6 Bringing Your Boston Terrier Home

*Photo Courtesy of
Jessica Goff Lance Bushard*

ty. Record the weight for yourself so you can see how quickly the puppy is growing. Ask your vet what a healthy weight is at each stage, and record that as well. Boston Terriers grow unbelievably fast during the first year, but you should still make sure your dog isn't gaining more weight than is healthy. During the 2010s, there was a trend of fat Boston Terriers because of how "cute" they looked waddling. This is not only bad for your Boston Terrier's health, it will reduce his life span. To ensure your Boston Terrier stays healthy, you need to know what your dog's weight is upon arrival, then you will have to monitor it over the course of your canine's life to ensure your dog remains healthy.

The vet will set the date for the next set of shots, which will likely happen not too long after your puppy arrives. When it is time for his vaccinations, be prepared for a day or two of your puppy feeling under the weather.

Crate And Other Preliminary Training

"I recommend you use their crate as their bed so they feel comfortable there. Give them a favorite toy or some treats when they go in. Leave them in the crate for only a few minutes to start and work your way up to longer stays."

Markella Motz
Bly Mountain Bostons

As mentioned, training starts from the moment your Boston Terrier becomes your responsibility. Considering the fact that your dog may be stubborn, you want to start getting your pup used to the idea that you are in charge. This will help play against the Boston Terrier's headstrong nature. Don't expect training to eliminate the behavior, but you can at least let your new pup know what the hierarchy is.

Puppies younger than six months old shouldn't be in the crate for hours at a time. They will not be able to hold their bladders that long, so you need to make sure they have a way to get out and use the restroom in an acceptable place. If you get an adult dog that is not housetrained, you will need to follow the same rules.

Make sure that the door is set so that it doesn't close on your dog during his initial sniff of the crate. You don't want your Boston Terrier to get hit by the door as it is closing and scare him.

CHAPTER 6   Bringing Your Boston Terrier Home

STEPS TO INTRODUCING YOUR PUPPY TO THEIR CRATE

1. LET YOUR BOSTON TERRIER SNIFF THE CRATE.

Talk to him while he does this, using a positive, happy voice. Associate the first experience in the crate with excitement and positive emotions so that your dog understands it is a good place. If you have a blanket from the puppy's mother, put it in the crate to help provide an extra sense of comfort.

2. DROP A COUPLE OF TREATS INTO THE CRATE

if your canine seems reluctant to enter it. Do NOT force your dog into the crate. If your dog doesn't want to go all the way into this strange little space, that is perfectly fine. It has to be his decision to enter so that it isn't a negative experience.

3. FEED YOUR DOG IN THE CRATE FOR A WEEK OR TWO.

This will help create some positive emotions with the crate, as well as helping you to keep the food away from other pets if you have them.
a.   If your dog appears comfortable with the crate, put the food all the way at the back of the crate.
b.   If not, place the food bowl in the front, then move it further back in the crate over time.

4. START CLOSING THE DOOR

once your dog appears to be eating comfortably in the crate. When the food is gone, open the crate immediately.

5. LEAVE THE DOOR CLOSED

for longer periods of time after your dog has eaten. If your pup begins to whine, you have left your Boston Terrier in the crate for too long.

6. CRATE YOUR DOG FOR LONGER PERIODS OF TIME

once your dog shows no signs of discomfort in the crate when he is eating. You can start to train him to go into the crate by simply saying "crate" or "bed," then praise your dog to let him know that he has done a great job.

Repeat this for several weeks until your dog feels comfortable in the crate. Doing this several times each day can help your dog to learn that everything is all right and that the crate is not a punishment. Initially, you will be doing this while you are still at home or when you go out to get the mail. As soon as your puppy can make it for half an hour without whining while you're out of the room, you can start leaving your pup alone while you are gone, keeping the time to no more than an hour in the beginning.

Once your dog understands he is not supposed to tear up your home, the crate training is complete.

The focus during these first few weeks is to start housetraining and minimize any undesirable behavior. Training from the start is vital, but don't take your new puppy to any classes just yet. This is because most puppies have not had all of the necessary shots, and good trainers will not allow them in classes until the full first round of shots is complete. Chapters 10 and 12 provide a closer look at the different kinds of training you should begin and how to follow through after the first few weeks.

First Night Frights

That first night is going to be scary to your little Boston Terrier puppy. As understandable as this may be, there is only so much comfort you can give your new family member. Just like with a baby, the more you respond to cries and whimpering, the more you are teaching a puppy that negative behaviors will provide the desired results. You will need to be prepared for a balancing act to provide reassurance that things will be all right while keeping your puppy from learning that crying gets your attention.

Create a sleeping area just for your puppy near where you sleep. The area should have the puppy's bed tucked safely into a crate. It offers him a safe place to hide so that he can feel more comfortable in a strange new home. The entire area should be blocked off so that no one can get into it (and the puppy can't get out) during the night. It should also be close to where people sleep so that the puppy doesn't feel abandoned. If you were able to get a blanket or pillow that smells like the mother, make sure this is in your puppy's space. Consider adding a little white noise to cover unfamiliar sounds that could scare your new pet.

Your puppy will make noises over the course of the night. Don't move the puppy away, even if the whimpering keeps you awake. If you give in, over time the whimpering, whining, and crying will get louder. Being moved away from people will only scare the puppy more, reinforcing the anxiety he

CHAPTER 6 Bringing Your Boston Terrier Home

feels. During the night, your puppy is not whimpering because he's been in the crate too long; he's scared or wants someone to be with him – he's probably never been alone at night before arriving at your home. Spare yourself some trouble later by teaching the puppy that whimpering doesn't always work to get him out of the crate. Over time, simply being close to you at night will be enough to reassure your puppy that everything will be all right.

Don't let your puppy into your bed until he is fully housetrained. Once a Boston Terrier learns that the bed is accessible, you can't train him not to hop up on it. And if he isn't housetrained, you'll need a new bed in the near future.

Puppies will need to go to the bathroom every two to three hours, and you will need to get up during the night to make sure your puppy understands that he is to always go to the bathroom either outside or on the pee pad. If you let it go at night, you are going to have a difficult time training him that he cannot go in the house later.

CHAPTER 7
The Multi-Pet Household

Boston Terriers may be intelligent, but they are lovers, not fighters. They are rarely the problem when introducing them to new dogs – they pretty much want to befriend everyone. As long as your dogs love other dogs too, it will be incredibly easy to get them accustomed to each other. Even if that is the case, the introductions need to follow the same precautions as those of a less friendly dog. You want to ensure all of the dogs present feel comfortable, including being on neutral ground during that first meeting. You should not introduce them at your home, no matter how friendly your dogs are, or how friendly your new dog is. After that introduction, it will almost certainly be easy to start integrating your new dog into the fuzzy part of the family.

Proper socialization is important for Boston Terriers if you bring home a puppy. Having a dog already in your home can help your puppy become socialized earlier, as well as teach your puppy how things work in your home. It is likely that your Boston Terrier will pick up on your other dog's listening to you, which could make it easier to get the Boston Terrier to listen – another fantastic benefit of having a friendly, intelligent dog. This works both ways though. If your current dog or dogs have any undesirable behaviors, you may want to try to work those out before your puppy arrives, too – you don't want your Boston Terrier learning bad habits.

Introducing Your New Puppy To Your Other Pets

"The best way to introduce your new puppy to pets already in the household is to use a crate. Put the puppy in the crate and let the other pets check them out. Then reverse the role and put the other pets in a crate and let the puppy check them out and their new surroundings. If more than one pet already in the household then only let one out at a time to get to know each other. Don't just walk in the door and set the puppy down with other pets."

Linda Reaves
Bama's Hurricane Creek Kennel

CHAPTER 7   The Multi-Pet Household

Always introduce all new dogs to your current dog or dogs, regardless of age, in a neutral place away from your home. Even if you have never had problems with your current dog, you are about to change his world. Select a park or other public area where your dog will not feel territorial and plan to introduce your dog to the puppy there. This gives the animals the opportunity to meet and get to know each other before entering your home together.

When introducing your dog and puppy, make sure you have at least one other adult with you so there's a person to manage each canine. If you have more than one dog, then you should have one adult per dog. This will make it easier to keep all of the dogs under control. Even the best dogs can get overly excited about meeting a puppy. One of the people who needs to be there is the person who is in charge of the pets in your home (or people if you have more than one person in charge). This helps establish the pack hierarchy.

Don't hold your puppy when the dogs meet. While you may want to protect the puppy and make him feel comfortable by holding him, it has the opposite effect. Your puppy will likely feel trapped, with no way to escape. Being on the ground means that the puppy can run if he feels the need to. Stand near the puppy with your feet a little bit apart. That way, if the puppy decides he needs to escape he can quickly hide behind your legs.

Watch for raised hackles on your dog. The puppy and each dog should have a few minutes to sniff each other, making sure that there is always some slack in the leash. This helps them feel more relaxed since they won't

Photo Courtesy of Angie Primeaux

Photo Courtesy of Carla Flickinger

feel like you are trying to restrain them. Your dog will probably either want to play or will simply ignore the puppy.

- If they want to play, just be careful that the dog doesn't accidentally hurt the puppy.
- If the dog ends up ignoring the puppy after an initial sniff, that is fine too.

If your dog's hackles are up or if he is clearly unhappy, keep them apart until your dog seems more comfortable with the situation. Don't force the meeting.

The introduction could take a while, depending on individual dog personalities. The friendlier and more accepting your dog is, the easier it will be to incorporate your new puppy into the home. For some dogs a week is enough time to start feeling comfortable together. For other dogs, it could take a couple of months before they are fully accepting of a new puppy. Since this is a completely new dynamic in your household, your current dog may not be pleased with you bringing a little bundle of energy into his daily life. This is enough to make anyone unhappy, but especially a dog that has grown accustomed to a certain lifestyle. The older your dog is, the more likely it is that a puppy will be an unwelcome addition. Older dogs can get cranky around a puppy that doesn't understand the rules or doesn't seem to know when enough is enough. The

CHAPTER 7   The Multi-Pet Household

goal is to make your puppy feel welcome and safe, while letting your older dog know that your love for him is just as strong as ever.

Once your new family member and the rest of the canine pack start to get acquainted and feel comfortable with each other, you can head home. As they enter the house, they will have a bit more familiarity with each other, making your current dogs feel more comfortable with the new addition to the family.

Once you are home, take the dogs into the yard and remove the leashes. You will need one adult per dog, including the puppy. If they seem to be all right or the dog is indifferent to the puppy, you can let your dog inside, re-leash the puppy, and keep the puppy on the leash as you go inside.

Put the puppy in the puppy area when the introductions are done.

Introducing An Adult Dog To Other Animals

You always need to approach the introduction and first few weeks with caution. The new adult Boston Terrier will need his own stuff in the beginning, and should be kept in a separate area when you aren't around until you know that there won't be any fighting. If your dogs don't have much interest in being the boss and enjoy playing rough, it will take less time for your new Boston Terrier to fit into the pack.

Plan for the introduction to take at least an hour. It probably won't take that long, but you must make sure that all of the dogs are comfortable during the introduction. Since the dogs are all adults, they will need to move at their own pace.

Follow the same steps to introduce your current dogs with your new dog as you would with a puppy.

- Start on neutral territory.

- Have one adult human per dog present at the introduction (this is even more important when introducing an adult canine).

- Introduce one dog at a time – don't let several dogs meet your new Boston Terrier at the same time. Having multiple dogs approaching all at once in an unfamiliar environment with people the Boston Terrier doesn't know very well – you can probably see how this can be nerve-racking for any new dog.

Unlike with a puppy, make sure to bring treats to the meeting of two adults dogs. The animals will respond well to the treats, and you will have a way to quickly distract all of the dogs if they are too tense with each other.

> **FUN FACT**
> **A Dog by Any Other Name**
>
> Boston Terriers were initially called "round heads" or "bull terriers" by their first group of fans, the American Bull Terrier Club. There was already another breed known as the Bull Terrier, however, so the club changed the name to the Boston Terrier.

During the introduction, watch the Boston Terrier and your dogs to see if any of them raises his hackles. This is one of the first really obvious signs that a dog is uncomfortable. If the Boston Terrier's hackles are up, back off the introductions for a little bit. Do this by calling your current dog back first. This is also when you should start waving treats around. Avoid pulling on the leashes to separate the dogs. You don't want to add physical tension to the situation because that could trigger a fight. Treats will work for all dogs present in the beginning, and your other dogs should be able to respond to your calling their names.

If any of the dogs are showing their teeth or growling, call your dog back and give the dogs a chance to settle down first. Use the treats and a calming voice to get them to relax. You want all the dogs to feel comfortable during the first meeting, so you can't force the friendship. If they seem uncomfortable or wary at first, you will need to let them move at their own pace.

Older Dogs And Your Boston Terrier

If your current dog is older, keep in mind that puppies are energetic and likely to keep trying to engage the older dog in play. This can be very trying for your older canine. Make sure that your older dog isn't getting too tired of the puppy's antics because you don't want your puppy to learn to snap at other dogs. Watch for signs that your older dog is ready for some alone time, some time alone with you, or just a break from the puppy.

Once your Boston Terrier is ready to leave the puppy area for good, you will still want to make sure that your older dog has safe places to go to be alone in case he just doesn't feel up to being around a spry young thing. This will reduce the likelihood that your puppy will be repeatedly scolded and therefore learn to be wary of older dogs.

Even if you adopt an adult Boston Terrier, they tend to like to play rough with other dogs. This can be a problem with older dogs, so make sure that your dog's golden years aren't marred by a new canine that has rules that don't make sense to your older dog and wants to play in a way your older dog can't.

CHAPTER 7 The Multi-Pet Household

Dog Aggression And Territorial Behaviors

When out of the home, Boston Terriers are really not a problem. Some people have classified the breed as aggressive because they will snap at dogs that get too enthusiastic or in-your-face. This is a breed that likes to be in charge and is quite independent. Just as you would not react well to someone crowding your personal space and being too friendly, a Boston Terrier may snap when another dog invades his space. This is not a true act of aggression, more of a warning that the dog is acting in a way that the Boston Terrier doesn't like. Once the dog backs off, your Boston Terrier will probably entirely lose interest. This is different from a dog that is aggressive because an aggressive dog will continue to try to get to the other dog. A Boston Terrier just wants to have his own personal space. Once that is achieved, he probably will go back to acting normal. It is your job to make sure other people know to keep their overeager dogs from getting too up close and personal with your dog.

Do not use choke chains or other negative reinforcers on your Boston Terrier. Not only do those hurt your dog, but a Boston Terrier does not react well to negative reinforcement because he thinks for himself. What you teach your Boston Terrier with these types of restraints is that you don't know what you are doing and are using things to try to force your dog to behave in a certain way. What does work are treats and removal from any negative situation. Reward your dog for the good behavior, and the more often your dog does what you want him to do, the more often you reward him. Chapter 12 goes into how to train your Boston Terrier.

At home, you will need to be more careful. Despite his size, a Boston Terrier is not the kind of dog to back down, so if he feels that someone is challenging him or taking one of his toys, he may react aggressively. While he is young, it is easier to start to train against this kind of behavior, but an

Photo Courtesy of Autumn Narducci

older dog will need extra monitoring and should not be left alone with other pets or children. An older Boston Terrier has to learn how to be a part of the pack and the proper way to react to people playing with toys and other items. This is why it is essential to always be firm and consistent.

There are two primary types of aggression that you should monitor for in your dog.

- Dominance aggression is when your dog wants to demonstrate control over another animal or person. This kind of aggression is shown through the following behaviors in reaction to anyone going near the Boston Terrier's belongings (like toys or a food bowl):

  o Growling

  o Nipping

  o Snapping

  This is the behavior that the pack leader makes to warn others in the pack about touching his stuff. If your Boston Terrier reacts like this toward you, a family member, or another pet going close to his stuff, you must intervene immediately, correct him by saying "No," then lavish him with praise when he stops. You must consistently intervene whenever your Boston Terrier behaves in this manner.

  Do not let the Boston Terrier be alone with other people, dogs, or animals as long as any of this type of behavior is exhibited. He will push boundaries, and if you aren't there to intervene, he will likely try to show his dominance in your absence.

  You want to train your Boston Terrier not to react aggressively. Once you are sure the behavior has been eliminated, you can leave your dog and Boston Terrier alone for short periods of time, with you staying in another room or somewhere in close proximity, but out of sight. Over time, you can start to leave your pets alone when you go get the mail, then when you run errands. Eventually, you will be able to leave your Boston Terrier alone with other dogs without worrying that he or one of your other dogs will feel compelled to show dominance.

- Well socialized males are more interested in meeting and greeting other dogs. Unsocialized males can be aggressive and domineering. Females tend to be more predictable; they are more aloof even when properly socialized, but they are also less likely to be as aggressive or domineering when not socialized.

Your Boston Terrier will have to learn that the home is not just his. It belongs to people and the other dogs as well, and he is a part of the home, not the boss in your home.

CHAPTER 7   The Multi-Pet Household

Strong Natural Prey Drive

"Boston's are often good with other pets but should be introduced slowly. Especially with cats as their eyes can be scratched or damaged easily. Some Boston's can have a very strong prey drive so be sure you know your dog and how it will react before introducing a new pet."

Lorene Jones
Ta-Koda Boston Terriers

Part of the terrier's history is as a pursuer of pests around the home. This sticks with some Boston Terriers, which could make walking a little trickier. While you won't have to worry too much about your dog pulling you over in an attempt to get a squirrel or other small animal nearby, you will need to prepare to train your dog to be less focused on those small animals. You don't want him to break the leash or slip his collar and get loose.

You will also need to be careful about the introduction with cats, because of the chance that the cat will run. Boston Terriers will almost certainly see that as a sign that it is playtime, so they will pursue the cat. It isn't so much about catching the cat as just having fun, but that doesn't mean that the cat will be pleased. Puppies will probably be easier to introduce to cats because their ability to run will be hampered by their short legs. You will need to plan to socialize your Boston Terrier puppy with the cat long before the puppy is allowed to run free in the home. Always be present when they interact so that you can correct the puppy's behavior.

It is unlikely that the prey drive will be a problem with your current pets, but you will want to be careful with your Boston Terrier and any rodents you have. Keep the cages for rodents too high and away from anything that your dog could stand on. It isn't normal to have problems, but that doesn't mean it isn't possible. If you have other small animals, they will need to be kept in areas where your Boston Terrier cannot go. Rabbits, ferrets, and other pets typically are not trainable. Most small animals aren't able to learn not to run away, which your puppy will likely take as an invitation to play. Since smaller animals are usually in containers, this will make them less interesting to your Boston Terrier. It is when you are outside that you have to be more careful of your Boston Terrier's natural drive to chase. This means that you really should not allow your Boston Terrier off-leash without fencing. Even if you do have fencing, you will need to keep a close eye on your dog. If a small animal catches your Boston Terrier's attention, he may become focused on catching the creature.

Photo Courtesy of Tabitha Lynn

Feeding Time Practices

Your Boston Terrier puppy will be fed in the puppy space, so mealtime will not be a problem in the beginning. When you start to feed the puppy with the other dogs, you can use the following instructions to reduce the chance of territorial behavior with food.

Eventually, you can start feeding the dogs close together. It can take weeks to months, depending on the age of the Boston Terrier when he comes to your home. A puppy will require less time because he will be socialized with the dogs from an early age, making him less wary. That does not mean that he won't display territorial behavior, but it likely won't take long for him to start to feel comfortable eating near the rest of the pack.

For adult dogs, it could take longer, and you should not rush it. Let your dog learn to feel comfortable eating before you make changes, even small ones. Dogs of any breed can be protective of their food, depending on what they have been through; this is exacerbated in protective breeds like the Boston Terrier. Your Boston Terrier needs to feel assured that this protective behavior is not necessary around other dogs before he will eat without incident. That means letting his confidence and comfort build at his own pace.

CHAPTER 7 The Multi-Pet Household

5 STEPS TO ENSURE PEACEFUL EATING

1. SIMULTANEOUS BUT SEPARATE FEEDINGS

Feed your Boston Terrier at the same time as the other dogs, but in a different room. Keeping them separated will let your Boston Terrier eat without distractions or feeling that your other dogs will eat what is in his bowl. Make sure to feed your Boston Terrier in the same room each time, while the other dogs eat in their established room or rooms.

2. DON'T ALLOW FOOD SHARING

Keep your Boston Terrier and other dogs to their areas until they finish eating their food. Some dogs have a tendency to leave food in the bowl. Don't let them. They need to finish everything in the bowl because all food bowls will be removed as soon as the dogs are done eating.

3. STAY NEARBY, BUT DON'T DISTRACT

Make sure you have someone near your Boston Terrier so that he learns not to growl at people near the bowl. This will help to reduce stress when other dogs are around the food. If your dog demonstrates any aggression, immediately correct him by saying "No," then give him praise when he stops. Do not attempt to play with the food bowl, and make sure none of the kids play with it. Your dog needs to know that no one is going to try to steal his food.

4. SLOWLY MOVE THE DOGS CLOSER

Move the dogs closer together over a couple of weeks. For example, you can feed your current dog on one side of the door near the doorway and the Boston Terrier on the opposite side near the doorway.

5. FINALLY FEED IN THE SAME ROOM

After a month or two, you can feed the dogs in the same room, but with some distance between them. If your Boston Terrier starts to exhibit protective behavior with the other dogs, correct him, then praise him when he stops the behavior.

CHAPTER 8
The First Few Weeks

Your Boston Terrier puppy is probably going to spend most of his first week at his new home moving between being excited and being nervous when he isn't sleeping. After learning that your home is his home, your pup will start to exhibit more personality and interest in his new world. His curiosity will become something that helps him get over his anxiety, and then you will really have your work cut off for you. Housetraining is almost certainly going to be your biggest challenge (they are one of the slower breeds to housetrain), with boredom being a close second. Fortunately, it will be fairly easy to keep your dog happily entertained or too tired to get into much trouble during those first few weeks.

The bond you start to build in that first week will continue to develop over the first month. By the end of the first month, your pup should be sleeping through the night and may have a fairly good understanding of where to go to the bathroom. You will also have a pretty good understanding of your canine's personality, which will make it a lot easier to know how to comfort the puppy during his infrequent bouts of uncertainty.

The first month is when you really need to start paying attention to your puppy's emerging personality. With a Boston Terrier, this will probably be when you start to notice that he will pick a favorite person. This doesn't mean your dog doesn't love the rest of the family, but he will be more comfortable with one person. Don't take it personally if you aren't the chosen favorite. It could mean that the favorite will need to take training very seriously and more responsibility may fall on that person's shoulders. That does not absolve the rest of the family of caring for the dog. Just because he has a favorite doesn't mean that he doesn't love the family, and he's probably going to want everyone to be together, especially when it comes to walking or play time.

Like with all intelligent breeds, when it comes to training, the key during this time is to remain consistent; that means everyone, not just the person who is the favorite. Use what you learn about your puppy's personality to encourage good behavior.

CHAPTER 8 The First Few Weeks

Setting The Rules And Sticking To Them

Your puppy needs to understand the rules and know that you and your family mean them. A firm, consistent approach is best for both you and your dog. If you don't remain consistent, you are setting yourself and your Boston Terrier up for a lot of contention that will make everyone miserable. Once your canine learns to listen to you, training your Boston Terrier to do tricks will still be up to your dog's mood, but he will be more excited if he learns early on that you are in charge.

Photo Courtesy of Kelly Reardon White Valley Boston Terriers

Establish A No Jumping And No Mouthing Policy

"Like most puppies your Boston may want to chew on you while playing, but while this can be cute coming from a little puppy its not as cute in an adult dog. Discourage mouthing by providing lots of toys for your puppy."

Lorene Jones
Ta-Koda Boston Terriers

You will need to train your newest family member not to do certain puppy things, like nipping and jumping. Even if the breed isn't known for being aggressive and a Boston Terrier isn't likely to be able to knock you down, you still don't want him to learn bad habits. He is powerful enough to knock over small children if not properly trained. There is no malice behind this, just a desire to play. It's your responsibility to ensure that your dog learns how to play properly, which means not jumping up on people or nipping them.

Nipping

- One of the triggers for nipping is overstimulation, which can be one of the signs that your puppy is too tired to keep playing or training and you should put him to bed.
- Another trigger could be that your canine has too much energy. If this is the case, take your puppy outside to burn off some of his excess energy. At the same time, be careful not to over-exercise the puppy.

You need to be vigilant and immediately let your puppy know that nipping is not acceptable. Some people recommend using a water spritzer bottle and spraying the puppy while saying "No" after nipping. This is one of the few times when punishment may be effective, but you need to be careful that your dog doesn't associate it with anything other than the nipping.

Always tell your puppy "No" firmly whenever he is nipping, even if it is during playtime. You should also pull away and say "Ouch!" loudly to let your puppy know that his teeth are hurting you. This will help to establish the idea that nipping is bad and is never rewarded.

> **FUN FACT**
> **Presidential Pups**
>
> Boston Terriers have twice been owned by American presidents (though not while they were in office). President Warren G. Harding had a Boston Terrier named Hub, and President Gerald Ford had two Bostons called Spot and Fleck.

Chewing

All puppies chew to relieve the pain of teething. Chewing can be an expensive problem for your dog to have, but it is fairly common with this breed. Whether he is chewing your furniture, utensils, or clothing, you want to discourage this behavior as quickly as possible.

- Make sure you have toys for your Boston Terrier (whether adult or puppy) so that you can teach him what things are acceptable to chew on. Having a lot of available toys, and rotating those toys out, will help give your puppy or dog a variety of options.

Photo Courtesy of Deb Chorzempa

- If your puppy is teething, either refrigerate a couple of toys so they are cold, or give your puppy frozen carrots. The cold will help to numb the pain.

- Toys that are made either of hard rubber or hard nylon will be the best toys, particularly Kongs with kibble in them. You can even fill them with water and freeze them, which will give your puppy something cool to sooth the pain of teething.

For the most part, keeping your eye on your dog when he is not in his designated space will help you to quickly see when he is chewing on things he shouldn't. When this happens, say "No" firmly. If your dog continues to chew, put him back in his space. While he is in the space, make sure he has plenty of toys to chew on.

If you decide to use chew deterrents, such as different bitter and training sprays, be aware that some dogs will not care that an item tastes bad – they will chew anyway. Do not apply these deterrents and then leave your dog alone and expect him to just stop chewing. You need to see your dog's reaction before trusting that the bad habit is broken. Since the Boston Terrier is known for having separation anxiety, you will definitely want to find a way to alleviate the problem with chewing as quickly as possible so that your pup can be free to roam. However, putting gross flavors on stuff isn't as much of a deterrent for them as you may expect. It is best to try to train them not to chew over spraying your possessions and hoping that it works.

Jumping

Dogs typically jump on people when they first greet them. Use the following steps when you have a visitor (and if you can get someone who is willing to help, that will make the training that much easier).

STEPS TO ELIMINATING JUMPING UP ON VISITORS

1. PUT A LEASH ON THE DOG
when the person knocks on the door or rings the bell. The arrival of someone else will invariably excite most dogs, especially puppies.

2. LET THE PERSON IN
but do not approach the person with the puppy until he calms down.

3. REINFORCE PROPER BEHAVIOR WITH PRAISE
when the puppy keeps all four paws on the ground. Approach the visitor only after your Boston Terrier is calm.

4. IGNORE INCORRECT BEHAVIOR
Turn your body and ignore him when the puppy jumps up. Don't verbally correct him. Being completely ignored will be far more of a deterrent than any words you can say.

5. USE DISTRACTIONS TO HELP THEM CALM DOWN
Give your dog something to hold in his mouth if he does not settle down. Sometimes dogs just need a task to reduce their excitement. A stuffed animal or ball are ideal for distraction, even if your dog drops it.

6. GET LOW AND PET YOUR DOG
Having someone on his level will make him feel like he is being included. It also lets him sniff your face, which is part of a proper greeting. If your visitor is willing to help, this obvious acknowledgment can be a deterrent from jumping as the person is already on your dog's level.

Reward-Based Training Vs Discipline-Based Training

Other chapters detail the various aspects of training, but it is important to keep in mind just how much more efficient it is to train with rewards than with punishments, especially for an intelligent breed like the Boston Terrier. This will be a particular challenge as puppies can be exuberant and are easily distracted. It is important to remember that your puppy is young, so you need to keep your temper and learn when you need to take a break from training.

Several critical aspects that you will need to start working on during the first month:

- Housetraining (Chapter 9)
- Crate training (Chapter 6)
- Barking (Chapter 11)

Find out how much the breeder did in terms of housetraining and other such areas. The best breeders may even teach puppies one or two commands before they go home with you. If this is the case, keep using those same commands with your puppy so that the early training is not lost. This can help you establish the right tone of voice to use since the puppy will already know what the words mean and how to react to them. Once he understands that, he will more quickly pick up on other uses of that tone of voice as being the way you talk when you are training. It is another great way to let your little love know when you mean business versus when you want to play. These kinds of distinctions are easily picked up by a Boston Terrier and your dog will be more than happy to oblige.

Photo Courtesy of Berny Vraa

Separation Anxiety In Dogs And Puppies

Boston Terriers do not like to be left alone, and a majority of them can suffer from some pretty severe separation anxiety. You will want to plan to help your new dog know that everything will be just fine, even if you have to leave him alone for hours. This is where their intelligence can get them in trouble as they take out their anxiety and boredom on anything they can get their mouths on. Apart from making sure your dog is tired before you leave home, there are several ways you can prepare your puppy or dog for those longer days when they are left home alone.

In the beginning, keep the puppy's time alone to a minimum. The sounds of people moving around the house will help your Boston Terrier understand that the separation is not permanent. After the first week or so, alone time can involve you going out to get the mail, leaving the puppy inside by himself for just a few minutes. You can then lengthen the amount of time you are away from the puppy over a few days until the puppy is alone for 30 minutes or so at a time.

> **Here are some basic guidelines for when you first start to leave your puppy alone.**
> - Take the puppy out about 30 minutes before you leave.
> - Tire the puppy out with exercise or playtime so that your leaving is not such a big deal.
> - Place the puppy in the puppy area well ahead of when you go out to avoid having him associate the space with something bad happening.
> - Don't give your puppy extra attention right before you leave because that reinforces the idea that you give attention before something bad happens.
> - Avoid reprimanding your Boston Terrier for any behavior that happens while you are away. Reprimanding teaches him to be more stressed because it will seem like you come home angry.

If your Boston Terrier exhibits signs of separation anxiety, there are several things you can do to help make him comfortable during your absence.

- Chew toys can give your dog something acceptable to gnaw on while you are away.
- A blanket or shirt that smells like you or other family members can help provide comfort too. If you have worn the item and haven't gotten it very dirty, this is ideal, just make sure that you were not in

Photo Courtesy of Stephanie Hess

contact with any chemicals over the course of the day you wore it. You also need to make sure that your dog won't eat the item in your absence. Consider giving him something that you won't mind never wearing again, in case he shreds it to pieces.

- Leave the area well lit, even if it is during the day. Should something happen and you get home later than you intended to, you don't want your little guy to be in the dark.

- Turn on a stereo (classical music is best) or television (old-timey shows that don't have loud noises, like Mr. Ed or I Love Lucy) so that the house isn't completely quiet and unfamiliar noises are less obvious.

It will not take your Boston Terrier long to notice the kind of behaviors that indicate you are leaving. Grabbing your keys, purse, wallet, and other indications will quickly become triggers that can make your Boston Terrier anxious because he is going to quickly learn what these actions mean. Don't make a big deal out of it. If you act in a normal way, over time this will help your little one to understand that your leaving is fine and that everything will be all right.

How Long Is Too Long To Be Left Home Alone?

"Never leave your puppy alone in your home without supervision. If you can't be with them, then they will need to be confined to either a crate or an ex-pen."

Lorene Jones
Ta-Koda Boston Terriers

To help your dog, you should not leave your dog home alone for more than eight hours at a time. They tend to be alright between four and eight hours, but any longer than that and they can start to have problems. This really isn't a breed you should get if you have to work long hours on a regular basis or if there won't be someone home more often than not.

One of the problems in the beginning is that your dog will need to be in a crate, and that means he will be crated for the entire time you are gone. Initially, this time should be very short. As your dog becomes housetrained and more trustworthy, your goal should be to allow your dog to be out of the crate so that it doesn't feel like a punishment. Your companion will not do well being trapped in a crate for hours at a time. You need to find some good mental games or things that your pup can do while you are gone to keep your Boston Terrier from being destructive. This is also why it is vital to ensure that you have your home properly prepared prior to your dog's arrival, especially if you get an adult Boston Terrier. Once your dog is crate trained and you start trying to leave him alone for longer periods of time, you want to make sure any destructive urges are put in check as much as possible.

Photo Courtesy of Autumn Narducci

CHAPTER 8   The First Few Weeks

Don't Overdo It, Physically Or Mentally

"Get lots of toys and play with your new pup! It helps to curb unwanted behavior early on by just tiring them out. But don't play tug of war to rough, it can be damaging to their sensitive large eyes, as a young pup."

Markella Mot
Bly Mountain Bostons

A tired puppy is a lot like a tired toddler; you have to keep the little guy from becoming exhausted or overworking those little legs. You need to be careful about harming your puppy's growing bones. Your pup is probably going to think that sleep is unnecessary, no matter how tired he is. It is up to you to read the signs that tell you when to stop all activities and put your pup to bed or take a break.

Training needs to be conducted in increments of time that your puppy or dog can handle. Be careful that you aren't pushing the training past the puppy's concentration threshold or that you aren't discouraging your adult dog with commands that are too advanced for him. If you continue training past your puppy's energy levels, the lessons learned are not going to be the ones you want to teach your dog. At this age, training sessions don't need to be long, they just need to be consistent.

Walks will be much shorter during that first month. When you go out, stay within a few blocks of home. Don't worry – by the month's end, your puppy will have a lot more stamina so you can enjoy longer walks and short trips away from home if needed. By the end of the first year you should be able to go for a short jog, depending on the advice from your vet. You can also do a bit of running on the leash in the yard if your puppy has a lot of extra energy. This will help your Boston Terrier learn how to behave on the leash while running. Puppies have a tendency to want to attack the leash because it is a distraction from running freely.

Just because your puppy can't take long walks initially doesn't mean that he won't have plenty of energy. Daily exercise will be essential, with the caveat that you need to make sure your puppy isn't doing too much, too soon. Staying active will help him to not only be healthy, but keep him mentally stimulated. You will quickly realize just how sedentary you have been if you have never had a dog before because you will be on the move almost all of the time the puppy is awake.

CHAPTER 9
Housetraining

Housetraining a puppy isn't really any more difficult or time consuming than potty training a toddler, and it is going to be about that difficult to train your Boston Terrier. Part of what you will need to do is to set a schedule and then not deviate from it. Your new family member will want a clean area and will quickly learn to let you know when he needs to go.

Using a leash can be helpful in ensuring that your puppy learns when and where to go, but there will still be challenges as you try to convince your puppy that there is a designated place to use the bathroom and it isn't in the home.

Make sure to consistently apply these two rules.

1. Never let the puppy roam the home alone – he should always be in the dedicated puppy space when you aren't watching him. Your Boston Terrier won't be pleased with the idea of being in a soiled crate, so that is a deterrent from doing his business when you are not around. He may not take the same approach to other areas of the home if he is left free to wander.

> **HELPFUL TIP**
> **Crate Training**
>
> Crate training is not only helpful for house-training, but it's also critical to set dogs up for success as adults. Even if you don't intend to keep your Boston in a crate when you leave him home alone, it's crucial that you teach your Boston to be comfortable in a crate. That's because he is likely to encounter a crate or kennel at some point in his life—at the groomer, vet, or boarding facility, for example—and your Boston may hurt himself trying to escape if you haven't taken the time to get him used to spending time in a crate.

2. Give your puppy constant, easy access to the locations where you plan to housetrain him. You will need to make frequent trips outside as your puppy learns where to do his business, particularly if constant access to a place to use the restroom isn't possible. When you go out, put a leash on your puppy to make sure you make a point of where in the yard you want him to use the bathroom.

Always begin with a training plan, then be even stricter with yourself than you are with your puppy to keep that schedule. You are the key to the puppy learning where it is acceptable to do his business.

CHAPTER 9 Housetraining

Strap In – It's Going To Be A Challenge

"Always take your puppy out as soon as it wakes up from a nap, and after eating or drinking. Bostons can be difficult to housebreak so they require consistent outdoor time and lots praise when they get it right."

Lorene Jones
Ta-Koda Boston Terriers

While they are far from being the most difficult dog to train, Boston Terriers are definitely not among the easiest either. It is one of the most popular questions people have because of how surprisingly difficult they are to housetrain; they are loving, intelligent, and affectionate, which should make them easy to train. And it does for most types of training, just not housetraining. In part, it could be that people are more inclined to give in and let them get away with "accidents," but this just convinces them that you aren't serious about potty training.

There are many recommendations online, but ultimately the same, consistent process will work. You can try out some of the tips and, depending on the personality of your dog, those tips may help. This chapter focuses on the steps that are part of the foundation for succeeding.

Here's a quick list of the things that you are going to need to do, with more information provided a bit later in the chapter.

1. You should make sure that your Boston Terrier is crate trained (Chapter 6).

2. Watch for signs that your puppy is looking for a spot to go to the bathroom.

3. Set a schedule and always follow it. Your Boston Terrier will understand schedules and will start to expect the outings at the established times.

4. Praise is both an effective tool and much healthier than treats. As soon as your pup responds to praise, start to move away from treats.

5. Be patient. Every dog is different, so there is no way to predict how long it will take. Being patient will help a lot more than getting frustrated or upset. Boston Terriers react to human emotions, and housetraining will be that much more difficult if your dog starts to associate the training with negative emotions.

Inside Or Outside – Housetraining Options And Considerations

If your breeder has already started housetraining the puppy, stick to the method that the breeder used. This will increase the odds that housetraining will stick a little faster with your Boston Terrier.

You have the following housetraining options for your puppy:

- **Pee pads** – You should have several around the home for training, including in the puppy's area, but as far from his bed as possible.
- **Regular outings outside** – Organize these based on your puppy's sleeping and eating schedule.
- **Rewards** – You can use treats in the beginning, but quickly shift to praise.

In the beginning, the best way to housetrain your dog is to go out a lot of times, including at night, so that your puppy learns to keep all of his business outside. During the first few months, it is best to use a leash when you take the puppy out. This will help him learn to walk on a leash and keep him from getting distracted before he does his business.

A word of warning – don't start praising the puppy until he's done going to the bathroom. Interrupting him in mid-potty may make the puppy stop, increasing the odds that he will go again after you get back inside.

Setting A Schedule

"Be prepared to take your puppy outside to pee at the beginning about every hour, after every meal, and upon waking up. Be sure to always go outside with the puppy to confirm that they wet potty, and when they do give them lots of praise."

Maxine Uzoff
Oui Bostons

You need to keep an eye on your puppy and consistently have housetraining sessions:
- After eating
- After waking up from sleeping or each nap
- On a schedule (after it has been established)

Watch your Boston Terrier for cues like sniffing and circling, two common activities as a puppy searches for a place to go. Start tailoring your schedule around your puppy's unique needs.

Puppies have small bladders and little control in the early days. If you have to initially train your pup to go inside, there needs to be a single designated space with a clean pee pad in the puppy's area, and you need to stock up on the appropriate pads for the puppy. Then make sure you change those pads regularly so your puppy does not get accustomed to having waste nearby. The pads are better than newspaper and can absorb more. You will need to plan to transition to having him do his business outdoors as quickly as possible so that your Boston Terrier will learn that indoors is the wrong place to go.

Photo Courtesy of
Suzanne Maxine Uzoff
Oui Bostons

CHAPTER 9 Housetraining

Choosing A Location

A designated restroom space can help make the experience of housetraining easier because your Boston Terrier will begin to associate one area of the yard for that one purpose, rather than sniffing around until he finds a choice spot. Having him go in one spot regularly will also make cleanup much simpler too; that way you can continue to use the whole yard instead of having to worry about stepping in waste.

When you are out for walks is the perfect time to train your puppy to go to the bathroom. Between walks and the yard, your puppy will come to see the leash as a sign that it is time to relieve his bladder, which could become a Pavlovian response.

Make sure that you pay attention to your puppy the entire time you are outside. You need to make sure that he understands the purpose of going outside is to go to the bathroom. Do not send your puppy outside and assume that he's done what you wanted him to do. Until there are no more accidents in the home, you need to verify that your puppy isn't losing focus while he is outside.

Keyword Training

"Consistency is key! Use the same door to take your puppy out and use one word for going out (Potty or outside etc..) using more words confuses them. One word in any training works best."

Linda Reaves
`Bama's Hurricane Creek Kennel

All training should include keywords, even housetraining. You and all members of the family should know what words to use when training your dog where to go to the bathroom, and you should all be using those words consistently. If you have paired an adult with a child, the adult should be the one using the keyword during training.

To avoid confusing your puppy, be careful not to select words that you often use inside the home. Use a phrase like "Get busy" to let your puppy know it's time to get to work, not something that involves the word bathroom or potty – these are words that you will probably say inside, which could trigger him to go when you don't mean for him to go. "Get busy" is not a phrase most people use in their daily routine, so it is not something you are likely to say when you don't mean for your puppy to use the bathroom.

Once your puppy learns to use the bathroom based on the command, make sure he finishes before offering praise or rewards.

Reward Good Behavior With Positive Reinforcement

Positive reinforcement is very effective. In the beginning, take a few pieces of kibble with you when you are teaching your puppy where to go, both inside and outside the home. Learning that you are the one in charge will help teach your Boston Terrier to look to you for cues and instructions.

Part of being consistent with training means lavishing the little guy with praise whenever your puppy does the right thing. If you gently lead your puppy to the area on a leash without any other stops, it will gradually become obvious that your Boston Terrier should go there to use the bathroom. Once you get outside, encourage your pup to go when you get to the place in the yard that is intended to be his bathroom spot. As soon as he does his business, give him immediate and very enthusiastic praise. Pet your puppy as you talk to let the little guy know just how good the action was. Once the praise is done, return inside immediately. This is not playtime. You want your puppy to associate certain outings with designated potty time.

While praise is far more effective for Boston Terriers, you can also give your puppy a treat after a few successful trips outside. Definitely do not make treats a habit after each trip because you do not want your Boston Terrier to expect one every time he does his business. The lesson is to go outside, and the puppy can learn that such outings may include treats.

The best way to train in the first month or two is to go out every hour or two, even at night. You will need to set an alarm to wake you within that time to take the puppy outside. Use the leash to keep the focus on using the bathroom, give the same enthusiastic praise, then immediately return inside and go to bed. It is difficult, but your Boston Terrier will get the hang of it a lot faster if there isn't a long period between potty breaks. Over time, the pup will need to go out less frequently, giving you more rest.

If your Boston Terrier has an accident, it is important to refrain from punishing the puppy. Accidents are not a reason to punish – it really reflects more on your training and schedule than on what the puppy has learned. That said, accidents are pretty much an inevitability. When it happens, tell your puppy, "No. Potty outside!" and clean up the mess immediately. Once that is done take the puppy outside to go potty. Of course, if your puppy doesn't go, he doesn't get any praise.

CHAPTER 9   Housetraining

Photo Courtesy of Blaire Pellerin

Cleaning Up

Clean up any messes in the home as soon as you find them. Unless you see your puppy using the bathroom in the home, there is no point in negative reinforcement. Your dog will simply learn to hide his mess to avoid being punished. Take the dog outside instead and see if he will use the bathroom. If someone is home, it is best to clean up the mess as quickly as possible. Spend a bit of time researching what kinds of cleaner you want to use, whether generic or holistic. For example, you will likely want to get something with an enzyme cleaner. Enzymes help to remove stains by speeding up the chemical reaction of the cleaner with the stain. It also helps to remove the smell faster, reducing the odds that your dog will continue to use the same place. Boston Terriers don't have an issue with marking their territory, especially if they are properly trained, but you may want to discourage dogs that are visiting from claiming areas where your puppy has had accidents. Enzyme cleaners are the best for cleaning up puppy accidents.

Pay attention to when these accidents happen and determine if there is a commonality between them. Perhaps you need to add an additional trip outside for your puppy or should make a change in his walking schedule. Or maybe there is something that is startling your dog, causing an accident.

CHAPTER 10
Socialization

"Socializing with other pets should be done cautiously at first, especially around larger dogs and cats. Keep in mind those large eyes and flat face make your new puppy very fragile. Slowly but surely most Bostons do wonderfully around other pets of all sizes."

Markella Motz
Bly Mountain Bostons

CHAPTER 10 Socialization

Socialization for Boston Terriers is incredibly easy because they are such an affable, gregarious breed. However, just because it will be easy doesn't mean that you can just "let it happen," because socialization is something that needs to be done cautiously. Their even, fun-loving temperament will make it easy, but you still want to approach socialization with caution to ensure that it is a positive experience.

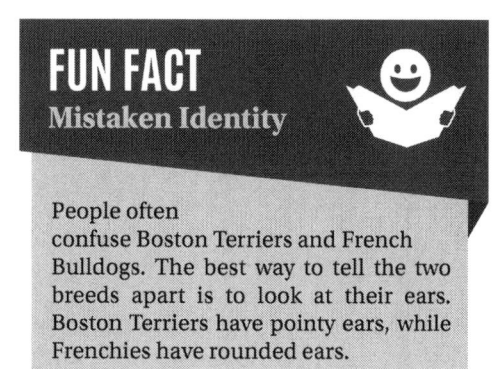

> **FUN FACT**
> **Mistaken Identity**
>
> People often confuse Boston Terriers and French Bulldogs. The best way to tell the two breeds apart is to look at their ears. Boston Terriers have pointy ears, while Frenchies have rounded ears.

Like any dog, Boston Terriers can be bossy, possessive, and jealous, though they aren't known for it. Sometimes the terrier or bulldog does come out, and then the experience can be a little less than enjoyable. If you start early, you can nip this in the bud, making it fun for both you and your pup. It could be a bit more of a challenge if you get an adult that hasn't been properly socialized.

Socialization allows your Boston Terrier puppy to learn that it can be a lot of fun to play with people you invite into your home and dogs that you encounter out on your walks. To make sure the best in your Boston Terrier's personality comes out, you have to plan to start socialization from a very early age.

Remember that your puppy will need to have all of his vaccinations before being exposed to other dogs.

Socialization Can Make Life Easier In The Long Run

All dogs need socialization, but intelligent breeds have more analytical minds, so you want them to learn as early as possible that most of the time the world is safe and that other people and animals usually don't pose a threat. Even with a breed as affable and loving as the Boston Terrier, if you neglect socialization, you and your dog may have be less friendly than his full potential.

It will also help you for your puppy to learn that acting in a dominant, aggressive way is not acceptable.

The benefit of early socialization is that it can make life that much more enjoyable for everyone involved, no matter what the situation is. A socialized dog will approach the world from a much better place than a dog that is not socialized.

Greeting New People

Training your Boston Terrier how to treat visitors may take a little longer because he may not be in the mood for any social interaction – and people are going to want to pet your adorable little dog. It will be just as important to let people know how to interact with your dog as it is to train your dog how to interact with visitors. Let your visitors know to leave the dog alone if the dog is not showing any interest in an introduction.

Puppies will likely enjoy meeting new people, so make sure to invite people over to help socialize your canine family member. To introduce your puppy to a new person, try one of these methods:

1. Try to have your puppy meet new people daily, if possible. This could be during walks or while you are doing other activities where you get out of the house. If you can't meet new people daily, try for at least 4 times a week.

2. Invite friends and family over, and let them spend a few minutes just giving the puppy attention. If your puppy has a favorite game or ac-

Photo Courtesy of Jason Pichler

CHAPTER 10 Socialization

Photo Courtesy of Jen Buck

tivity, let people know so that they can play with him. This will win the little guy over very quickly and teach him that new people are fun and safe.

3. Once your puppy is old enough to learn tricks (after the first month – don't try to teach him tricks immediately), have your little friend demonstrate the tricks for visitors. This will be really important as your puppy gets bigger because a lot of people are nervous around dogs of any size. A display of tricks helps them see that your dog is just as clownish and playful as other dogs.

4. Avoid crowds for the first few months. When your puppy is several months to a year old, attend some dog-friendly events so that your pup can learn not to be uncomfortable around a large group of people.

Photo Courtesy of Deb Chorzempa

CHAPTER 10   Socialization

Greeting New Dogs

Chapter 7 covers the introduction of your new Boston Terrier with your other dogs, but meeting other dogs is a little different. Most dogs will bow and sniff each other during an introduction. Watch for the same signs of aggression covered in Chapter 7, such as raised hackles and bared teeth. Bowing, high tail, and perked ears usually mean that your Boston Terrier is excited about meeting the dog. If your Boston Terrier is making noises, watch for the signs of aggression to make sure that the sounds are of play, not unease.

According to the Boston Terrier Society, about a third of Boston Terriers have been reported to be aggressive toward other dogs (none of them were aggressive to people). In case your Boston Terrier is aggressive, you want to train him early so that this isn't an issue. The best way to do that is with playdates at a neutral place. This will remove any jealousy about sharing toys or territorial tendencies.

Don't let your Boston Terrier jump up on other dogs. If he does, immediately say "No," to let him know that is not acceptable behavior. This can become a way of showing dominance, which you really don't want with your pup, even if it is just play in the beginning.

The Importance Of Continuing Socialization

"This is a lively breed as stated in the AKC Boston Terrier standard, so play time is important and going on leashed walks is good as it helps establish good social and learning experiences and builds a level of comfort to be around other people, places, and things."

Maxine Uzoff
Oui Bostons

Even friendly dogs need to be socialized. Making sure the puppy gets exposure to other people and other dogs is going to be important to keep him from getting too aggressive or dominant. This doesn't mean forcing him into interaction, but joining classes and setting up playdates will give your dog a reason to be excited about meeting other dogs.

Photo Courtesy of Suzanne Maxine Uzoff Oui Bostons

You don't have to leave home though if you don't want to. Have family and friends visit regularly, especially bringing their dogs along, so that your Boston Terrier has constant reminders that his home is a welcoming place, not somewhere that he needs to exert his dominance. You don't want your pup to feel that the outside world is fine, but that he can be a little terror at home.

Socializing An Adult Dog

Sometimes an adult dog will be too set in his ways to change, particularly if your dog is in his golden years. However, most adult dogs can be socialized as long as you make it your top priority (along with training). If you aren't prepared to be very patient with your Boston Terrier adult, then it is best not to adopt an adult. There is a chance that your Boston Terrier won't be as friendly with other dogs, even if he seems to be alright with other dogs at the rescue facility. Before you can begin to socialize your dog, you need to make sure he already knows some basic commands and that you have him under control before any introductions are made.

Socializing an adult canine requires a lot of time, dedication, gentle training, and a firm approach. You may be lucky enough to get an adult that is already well socialized. However, that does not mean that you can be entirely relaxed. The dog may have had a bad experience with a particular breed of dog that no one knows about.

If you have problems with your adult dog, consult a behaviorist or specialized trainer.

CHAPTER 10   Socialization

5 TIPS FOR CONTINUED SOCIALIZATION

TIP 1 — MASTER THE BASIC COMMANDS

Your dog should be adept at the following commands before you work on socialization: *Sit, Down, Heel, Stay*. Stay is especially important because if your dog can remain in one place based on your commands, then he is demonstrating self-control, something that will be very helpful for socialization because you can override an aggressive impulse by activating the listening mode. When you go outside, you will need to be very aware of your surroundings, and be able to command your dog before another dog or person gets near.

TIP 2 — USE A SHORT LEASH ON WALKS

At the first sign of aggression, turn and walk in the opposite direction. Being aware of your surroundings will start to cue you into what your dog is reacting to so you can start training your dog not to react negatively.

TIP 3 — CHANGE DIRECTION

if you notice that your Boston Terrier is not reacting well to a particular person or dog approaching you. Avoidance is a good short term solution until you know that your dog is more accepting of the presence of these other dogs or people.
If you aren't able to take a different direction, tell your dog to sit, then block your dog's view. This can prove to be very challenging as your dog will try to look around you. Engage in training to get your dog to listen to you, taking his mind off of what is coming toward him.

TIP 4 — SCHEDULE PLAY DATES WITH FRIENDLY DOGS

Ask friends with friendly dogs to visit you, then meet in an enclosed space. Having one or two friendly dogs interact with your dog can help your Boston Terrier to see that not all dogs are dangerous or need to be put in their place. Having the dogs walk around the area together without a lot of interaction can help your dog learn that other dogs are usually just interested in enjoying the outside, so there is no reason to try to bully them.

TIP 5 — GET SPECIAL TREATS JUST FOR WALKS

If your dog is aggressive when walking, have him sit, and give him one of the special treats. Boston Terriers are food motivated, so this could be a perfect way of distracting your dog from whatever is making him feel protective. At the first snarl or sign of aggression, engage the training mentality and draw upon your dog's desire for those special treats. This method is slow, but it is reliable over time because your dog is learning that the appearance of strangers and other dogs means special treats, a positive experience, not a negative one. However, this does not train the dog to interact with those dogs. You can couple it with the fourth suggestion to get the best results.

CHAPTER 11
Training Your Boston Terrier

"Boston Terriers are generally fast to catch on during training but some can be stubborn and challenging. Consistency and repetition is key in the formative and training stage which most importantly includes praise as reward for following commands and cues that are given by owners and family."

Maxine Uzoff
Oui Bostons

Photo Courtesy of Jen Buck

Boston Terriers can be fantastic to train for many types of skills. They love playing, they love being around you, and they are incredibly enthusiastic about learning whatever you want to teach them. Their natural enthusiasm for doing new things and spending time with their people is all they need to make them happy. Their intelligence makes it easy to get through to them.

While training will get increasingly more enjoyable over time, it will be fairly slow going in the beginning as your dog will be quite excited for the interaction. You will need to be firm and consistent, as well as keeping the training sessions very short in the beginning. If you can give your pup patience in the beginning, you will find that it will pay off later.

CHAPTER 11 Training Your Boston Terrier

Benefits Of Proper Training

In addition to making socialization and general excursions easier, training could be a way of saving your dog's life. Understanding commands will help to stop your dog from running into the street or from responding to provocations from other dogs (or from acting as the aggressor). Training could also be a time saver in the event your dog gets away from you.

Training is a great way to bond with your dog. It gives you dedicated time together and helps you to understand your puppy's developing personality and to learn what kinds of rewards will work best for other tasks, like socialization.

The most enjoyable benefit of having a solid foundation for training is being able to train your dog to do so much more. This is a dog that can join you when you go out for picnics or for other outings, so you want to make sure your Boston Terrier is trained so that you can enjoy a full range of activities.

Choosing The Right Reward

"They can be very sensitive when scolded, just a stern voice is usually enough to send them cowering if in trouble. So be sure to never swat or physically punish a Boston. They really just only want to please you!"

Markella Motz
Bly Mountain Bostons

The right reward for a Boston Terrier will ultimately be love and affection. Treats are the easiest way of keying a puppy into the idea that performing tricks is a good behavior. Soon, though, you will need to switch to something that is a secondary reinforcer. Praise, additional playtime, and extra petting are all fantastic rewards for Boston Terriers. He will probably follow you around until you decide to just sit back and relax. Plopping down to watch a movie and letting your puppy sit with you is a great reward after an intense training session. Not only did your puppy learn, but you both now get to relax together.

If you would like your Boston Terrier to attach positive feedback with a sound, you can use a clicker. They are relatively inexpensive and will need to be used at the same time as you praise your puppy or dog. They are not necessary, but some trainers do use them.

Photo Courtesy of Lisa Mazurek

Name Recognition

Over time, many of us come up with multiple names for our dogs. Nicknames, joke names, and descriptions based on some of their ridiculous actions (it's why we love them) can all be used later. However, before you can train a dog, you have to make sure your dog understands his real name.

1. Get some treats and show one to your dog.
2. Say the dog's name, immediately say "Yes" (your dog should be looking at you when you speak), then give your dog a treat.
3. Wait 10 seconds, then show your dog a treat and repeat step 2.

Sessions shouldn't last longer than about five minutes because your dog will lose either focus or interest. Name recognition is something you can do several times over the day. After you have done this over five to ten sessions, the training will change a bit.

1. Wait until your dog isn't paying attention to you.
2. Call your dog. If the dog has a leash on, give it a gentle tug to get your dog's attention.
3. Say "Yes" and give the dog a treat when he looks at you.

During this time, do not speak your dog's name during corrections or for no real reason. This is because in the beginning, you need to get the dog to associate the name only with something very positive, like treats. This will more quickly program your dog to listen to you no matter what else is going on around him.

It is likely that your Boston Terrier will not require a lot of time before he recognizes his name.

Essential Commands

There are five basic commands that all dogs should know. These commands are the basis for a happy and enjoyable relationship with your dog. By the time your puppy learns all five of the commands, it will be more obvious what the correlation between the words you say and the expected actions are. This will clue the dog in to understanding new words in terms of expectation and will make it much easier to train him on the more complex concepts.

Photo Courtesy of
Kayla Hall

CHAPTER 11   Training Your Boston Terrier

Train your puppy to do the commands in the order they appear in this chapter. Sit is a basic command, and something all dogs already naturally do. Since dogs tend to sit often, it is the easiest one to teach. Teaching leave it and drop it is much more difficult, and it usually requires that the puppy fight an instinct or desire. Consider how much you give in to something you want to do when you know you shouldn't – that's pretty much what you are facing, but with a puppy. Quiet can be another difficult command as dogs (particularly puppies) tend to bark as a natural reaction to something. These two commands will take longer to teach, so you want to have the necessary tools already in place to increase your odds of success.

> **Here are some basic guidelines to follow during training.**
>
> - Include everyone in the home in the Boston Terrier training. The puppy must learn to listen to everyone in the household, and not just one or two people. A set training schedule may only involve a couple of people in the beginning, especially if you have children. There should always be an adult present for training, but including one child during training will help reinforce the idea that the puppy must listen to everyone in the house. It is also a good way for the parent to monitor the child's interaction with the puppy so that everyone plays in a way that is safe and follows the rules.
>
> - To get started, select an area where you and your puppy have no other distractions, including noise. Leave your phone and other devices out of range so that you keep your attention on the puppy.
>
> - Stay happy and excited about the training. Your puppy will pick up on your enthusiasm, and will focus better because of it.
>
> - Be consistent and firm as you teach.
>
> - Bring a special treat to the first few training sessions, such as pieces of chicken or small treats.

Sit

Start to teach sit when your puppy is around eight weeks old. Once you settle into your quiet training location:

1. Hold out a treat.

2. Move the treat over your puppy's head. This will make the puppy move back.

3. Say 'sit' as the puppy's haunches touch the floor.

Having a second person around to demonstrate this with your puppy will be helpful as they can sit to show what you mean.

Wait until your puppy starts to sit down and say sit as he or she sits. If your puppy finishes sitting down, give praise. Naturally, this will make your puppy incredibly excited and wiggly, so it may take a bit of time before he will want to sit again. When the time comes and the puppy starts to sit again, repeat the process.

It's going to take more than a couple of sessions for the puppy to fully connect your words with the actions. Commands are something completely new to your little companion. Once your puppy has demonstrated mastery over sit, start teaching down.

Down

Repeat the same process to teach this command as you did for sit.

1. Tell your dog to sit.
2. Hold out the treat.
3. Lower the treat to the floor with your dog sniffing at it. Allow your pup to lick the treat, but if he stands up, start over.
4. Say down as the puppy's elbows touch the floor, then give praise while letting your puppy eat the treat.

Wait until the puppy starts to lie down, then say down. If the Boston Terrier finishes the action, offer your chosen reward.

It will probably take a little less time to teach this command.

Wait until your puppy has mastered down before moving on to stay.

Stay

Stay is a vital command to teach because it can keep your puppy from running across a street or from running at someone who is nervous or scared of dogs. It is important that your dog has mastered sit and down before you teach stay. Learning this command is going to be more difficult since it isn't something that your puppy does naturally. Be prepared for it to take a bit longer.

1. Tell your puppy to either sit or stay.
2. As you do this, place your hand in front of the puppy's face.
3. Wait until the puppy stops trying to lick your hand before you begin again.

4. When the puppy settles down, take a step away. If your puppy is not moving, say stay and give a treat and some praise.

Giving your puppy the reward indicates that the command is over, but you also need to indicate that the command is complete. The puppy has to learn to stay until you say it is okay to leave the spot. Once you give the okay to move, do not give treats. Come should not be used as the okay word as it is a command used for something else.

Repeat these steps, taking more steps further from the puppy after a successful command.

Once your puppy understands stay when you move away, start training to stay even if you are not moving. Extend the amount of time required for the puppy to stay in one spot so that he understands that stay ends with the okay command.

When you feel that your puppy has stay mastered, start to train the puppy to come.

Come

This is a command you can't teach until the puppy has learned the previous commands. Before you start the training session, decide if you want to use come or come here for the command. Be consistent in the words you use.

This command is important for the same reason as the previous one. If you are around people who are nervous around dogs, or encounter a wild animal or other distraction, this command can snap your puppy's attention back to you.

1. Leash the puppy.

2. Tell the puppy to stay.

3. Move away from the puppy.

4. Say the command you will use for come and give a gentle tug on the leash toward you.

Repeat these steps, building a larger distance between you and the puppy. Once the puppy seems to understand it, remove the leash and start at a close distance. If your puppy doesn't seem to understand the command, give some visual clues about what you want. For example, you can pat your leg or snap your fingers. As soon as your puppy comes running over to you, offer a reward.

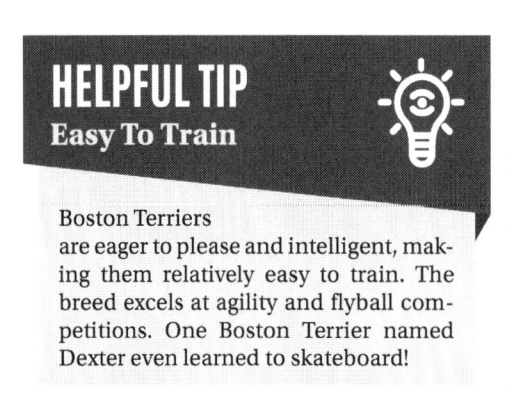

> **HELPFUL TIP**
> **Easy To Train**
>
> Boston Terriers are eager to please and intelligent, making them relatively easy to train. The breed excels at agility and flyball competitions. One Boston Terrier named Dexter even learned to skateboard!

Off

Although Boston Terriers are small, it's important to train your dog to get down or off something. This is not the same as teaching your dog not to jump on people (Chapter 8). This command is specifically to get your dog off furniture, off counters, and your lap (you may not always be in the mood for the flatulence or noise that comes with the Boston Terrier).

This is training that you will need to be prepared to do on the fly because you are training your dog to stop an action. This means you have to react to that undesirable action. Having treats on hand will be essential when you see your dog getting up on things you don't want him to be on.

1. Wait for your dog to put his paws on something that you don't want him on.
2. Say "Off" and lure him away with a treat that you keep just out of his reach.
3. Say "Yes" and give him a treat as soon as his paws are off the surface.

Repeat this every time you see the behavior. It will likely take at least half a dozen times before your dog understands he should not perform the action anymore. Over time, switch from treats to praise or playing with a toy.

Leave It

This is a difficult training command, but you need to teach your dog leave it for when you are out on a walk and want him to ignore other people or dogs.

1. Let your dog see that you have treats in your hand, then close it. Your fist should be close enough for your dog to sniff the treat.
2. Say "Leave it" when your dog starts to sniff your hand.
3. Say "Yes" and give your dog a treat when he turns his head away from the treats. Initially, this will probably take a while as your dog will want those treats. Don't continue to say "Leave it" as your dog should not be learning that you will give a command more than once. You want him to learn that he must do what you say the first time you say it, which is why treats are recommended in the beginning.

CHAPTER 11   Training Your Boston Terrier

If a minute or more passes after giving the command, you can then issue it again, but make sure your canine is focused on you and not distracted.

These sessions should only last about five minutes and it will take your dog some time to learn, as you are teaching him to ignore something he does naturally. When he starts to understand and looks away when you say leave it without spending much time sniffing, you can move on to more advanced versions of the training.

1. Leave your hand open so that your dog can see the treats.
2. Say "Leave it" when your dog starts to show interest (this will probably be almost immediately, especially since you won't have your hand closed, so be prepared).
    a. Close your fist if your dog continues to sniff or gets near the treats in your hand.
    b. Give your dog a treat from your other hand if he stops.

Repeat these steps until your dog finally stops trying to sniff the treats. When your dog seems to have this down, move on to the most difficult version of this command.

1. Place treats on the ground, or let your dog see you hide them, and stay close to those treats.
2. Say "Leave it" when your dog starts to show interest in sniffing the treats.
    a. Place a hand over the treats if he doesn't listen.
    b. Give him a treat from your hand if your dog does listen.

From here, you can start training while standing further from the treat with your dog leashed so you can stop him if needed. Then start to use other things that your dog loves, such as a favorite toy or another tempting treat that you don't usually give.

Drop It

This is going to be one of the most difficult commands you will teach your puppy because it goes against both your puppy's instincts and interests. Your puppy wants to keep whatever he has, so you are going to have to offer him something better instead. It is essential to teach the command early though, as your Boston Terrier could be very destructive in the early days. Furthermore, this command could save your pooch's life. He is likely to lunge at things that look like food when you are out for a walk and this command will get him to drop anything potentially hazardous that he picks up.

Start with a toy and a treat, or a large treat that your dog cannot eat in a matter of seconds, such as a rawhide. Make sure the treat you have is one that your puppy does not get very often so that there is motivation to drop the toy or big treat.

1. Give your puppy the toy or large treat. If you want to use a clicker too, pair it with the exciting treat that you will use to help convince your puppy to drop the treat.
2. Show your puppy the exciting treat.
3. Say Drop it and when he drops the treat or toy, tell him good and hand over the exciting treat while picking up the dropped treat or toy.
4. Repeat this immediately after your puppy finishes eating the exciting treat.

Photo Courtesy of Annette Hostetter Sundberg

You will need to keep reinforcing this command for months after it is learned because it is not a natural reaction. You should also start using food that your dog finds almost irresistible. This is one of those rare times when you must use a treat because your puppy needs something to convince him to drop a cherished toy, or more importantly, food that he shouldn't be eating.

Quiet

You want to ensure your pup doesn't become a nuisance, especially if you are in an apartment. Initially, you can use treats sparingly to reinforce quiet if your pup enjoys making noise.

1. When your puppy barks with no obvious reason, tell him to be quiet and place a treat nearby. It is almost guaranteed that the dog will fall silent to sniff the treat.

2. If your dog does fall silent, say good dog or good quiet.

It will not take too long for your puppy to understand that quiet means no barking.

If you want your Boston Terrier to be more of a watch dog, you will need to provide some guidance on when he should bark. For example, you can teach him to bark when people come to the door (you will need to get a friend to help you so that he doesn't bark when family arrives). Otherwise, you will want him to know that he shouldn't be randomly barking at birds at the window or squirrels running around in the yard.

Where To Go From Here

Boston Terriers are a breed that are fairly easy to train, so you may not need to take your dog to any classes. As often as not, they will be able to pick up on what you want to train without any other help. However, they will enjoy the extra socialization if you want to take them to a puppy or obedience class. For the Boston Terrier, these classes are really more to train you how to train them than it is for the dog. It is a safe environment and a great opportunity for you to both learn, and there will be an expert present to instruct you in the best way to teach your pup how to act.

Puppy Classes

Puppies can begin to go to puppy school as early as 6 weeks. This is the beginning of obedience training, but you will need to be careful about their interactions with other dogs until your puppy has completed his vaccinations. Talk with your vet about when is a good time to begin classes, or at least a safe time. Your vet may be able to recommend good puppy training classes in your area.

The primary purpose of these classes is socialization, which is really important for a breed like the Boston Terrier. Studies have shown that a third of puppies have minimal exposure to new people and dogs during the first 20 weeks of their life, which can make the outside world scarier. The puppy classes give you and your puppy a chance to learn how to meet and greet other people and dogs in a strictly controlled environment. Dogs that attend these classes are much friendlier and are less stressed about things like large trucks, loud noises, and visitors. They are also less likely to be nervous or suffer from separation anxiety.

It is also good training for you. In the same studies, people were better able to react appropriately when a puppy was disobedient or misbehaved, something that is absolutely essential when training a Boston Terrier. It teaches you how to train your puppy and how to deal with the emerging headstrong nature of your dog.

Many classes will help you with some of the basic commands, like sit and down. Look for a class that also focuses on socialization so that your puppy can get the most out of the class.

Obedience Training

After your puppy graduates from puppy school and understands most of the basics commands, you can switch to obedience classes. Obedience classes are more difficult, but it shouldn't be that much of a challenge for a Boston Terrier. Some trainers offer at home obedience training, but it is best to find a class so that your dog can continue socialization as a part of his training. If your puppy attends puppy classes, the trainers can provide you with the next classes that they recommend. Dogs of nearly any age can attend obedience training classes, though your dog should be old enough to listen (this is why there are puppy classes – dogs who are 20 weeks old or less are a different kind of training problem).

Obedience training usually includes the following:

- Teaching or reinforcing basic commands, like sit, stay, come, and down.
- How to walk without pulling on the leash.
- How to properly greet people and dogs, including not jumping on them.

CHAPTER 11   Training Your Boston Terrier

Obedience school is as much about training you as training your dog. It helps you learn how to train while getting your dog through basic commands and how to behave for basic tasks, like greetings and walking. Classes usually last between 7 and 10 weeks.

Ask your vet for recommendations. If your vet doesn't have any recommendations, take time to thoroughly research your options. Look at the following details when evaluating trainers:

- Are they certified, particularly the CPDT-KA certification?
- How many years have they been training dogs?
- Do they have experience with training Boston Terriers?
- Can you participate in the training? If the answer is no, do not use that trainer. You have to be a part of your dog's training because the trainer is not going to be around most of your dog's life. Therefore, your dog has to learn to listen to you.

Obedience training does not help with serious behavioral issues. If your dog has anxiety, depression, or other serious behavioral issues, you need to hire a trainer to help your dog work through those issues. Do your research to make sure your selected trainer is an expert, preferably with experience with intelligent, strong-willed dogs. If possible, find someone who has experience dealing with Boston Terriers.

Once your Boston Terrier has the basic commands down and has done well in obedience training, you can start to do other more enjoyable training. As long as your Boston Terrier did well in the classes, you should not need a trainer because your dog will listen to you. With a foundation for commands and a more active interest in learning more, this could be a great foundation for doing more – as long as your Boston Terrier is interested. By this point, you should be able to tell if your dog is interested, and you will definitely have more of an idea if you want to pursue more difficult training given your dog's personality.

CHAPTER 12
Nutrition

"Boston Terriers often snore, and can be gassy. The trick is to find the right food for your dog and avoid giving them human foods."

Lorene Jones
Ta-Koda Boston Terriers

Boston Terriers already have sensitive stomachs and a lot of gas to persuade you that you need to take their dietary needs very seriously. High-quality diets can help to reduce how much your dog gases you, but it is unlikely that you will be able to completely stop the smells. Being overweight isn't healthy for any dog, but it is particularly bad for the smaller breeds and all brachial dogs. It is easy for them to overeat though as they tend to be given extra food since they are so small and cute. Since your dog is always near you, it will be easy to think that throwing him the occasional fry is fine. As you will soon learn, his stomach probably won't agree.

CHAPTER 12   Nutrition

Why A Healthy Diet Is Important

Boston Terriers are very food motivated. Given that they have respiratory troubles because of their short snouts, you want to make doubly sure they don't get overweight. That will just make it harder for your dog to breathe, while making it harder for your friend to play with you.

You need to be aware of roughly how many calories your dog eats a day, including treats. Be aware of your dog's weight so you can see when he is putting on pounds. This will key you in to when you should adjust how much food your Boston Terrier eats a day, or change his food to something with more nutritional value, but fewer calories.

Always talk with your vet if you have concerns about your Boston Terrier's weight. You can also establish regular weight checks at home because they fit on home scales.

Dangerous Foods

Dogs can eat raw meat without having to worry about the kinds of problems a person will encounter. However, there are some human foods that could be fatal to your Boston Terrier. You should keep these foods away from all dogs:

- Apple seeds
- Chocolate
- Coffee
- Cooked bones (they can kill a dog when the bones splinter in the dog's mouth or stomach)
- Corn on the cob (the cob is deadly to dogs; corn off the cob is fine)
- Grapes/raisins
- Macadamia nuts
- Onions and chives
- Peaches, persimmons, and plums
- Tobacco (your Boston Terrier will not know that it is not a food and may eat it if it's left out)
- Xylitol (a sugar substitute in candies and baked goods)
- Yeast

In addition to these potentially deadly foods, there is a long list of things that your dog shouldn't eat. The Canine Journal has a lengthy list of foods (http://www.caninejournal.com/foods-not-to-feed-dog/) that should be avoided.

Canine Nutrition

The dietary needs of a dog are significantly different than a human's needs. People are more omnivorous than dogs, meaning they require a wider range of nutrients to be healthy. Canines are largely carnivorous, and protein is a significant dietary requirement. However, they need more than just protein to be healthy.

The following table provides the primary nutritional requirements for dogs.

Nutrient	Sources	Puppy	Adult
Protein	Meat, eggs, soybeans, corn, wheat, peanut butter	22.0% of diet	18.0% of diet
Fats	Fish oil, flaxseed oil, canola oil, pork fat, poultry fat, safflower oil, sunflower oil, soybean oil	8.0 to 15.0% of diet	5.0 to 15.0% of diet
Calcium	Dairy, animal organ tissue, meats, legumes (typically beans)	1.0% of diet	0.6% of diet
Phosphorus	Meat and pet supplements	0.8% of diet	0.5% of diet
Sodium	Meat, eggs	0.3% of diet	0.06% of diet

The following are the remaining nutrients dogs require, all of them less than 1% of the puppy's or adult's diet:

- Arginine
- Histidine
- Isoleucine
- Leucine
- Lysine
- Methionine + cystine
- Phenylalanine + tyrosine
- Threonine
- Tryptophan
- Valine
- Chloride

CHAPTER 12 Nutrition

Since so many human foods contain preservatives and salt, it is best to avoid giving your dog human foods with a lot of sodium.

Water is also absolutely essential to keeping your dog healthy. There should always be water in your dog's water bowl, so make a habit of checking it several times a day so that your dog does not get dehydrated.

Proteins And Amino Acids

Since dogs are carnivores, protein is one of the most important nutrients in a healthy dog's diet (although they should not eat meat nearly as exclusively as their close wolf relatives; their diets and needs have changed significantly since they became companions to humans). Proteins contain the necessary amino acids for your dog to produce glucose, which is essential for giving your dog energy.

CHAPTER 12   Nutrition

A lack of protein in your dog's diet will result in him being lethargic. His coat may start to look dull and he is likely to lose weight. Conversely, if your dog gets too much protein, your dog's body will store the excess protein as fat, meaning he will gain weight.

Meat is typically the best source of protein, and it is recommended since a dog's dietary needs are significantly different from a human's needs. However, it is possible for a dog to have a vegetarian diet as long as you ensure that your dog gets the necessary protein through other sources, and you will need to include supplemental vitamin D in his food. If you plan to feed your dog a vegetarian diet, talk to your vet first. It is incredibly difficult to ensure that a carnivore gets adequate protein with a vegetarian diet, especially puppies, so you will need to dedicate a lot of time to research and discussion with nutrition experts to ensure that your dog is getting the necessary proteins for his needs.

Fat And Fatty Acids

Most of the fats that your dog needs also come from meat, though seed oils can provide a lot of the necessary healthy fats too, with peanut butter being one of the most common sources. Fats are broken down into fatty acids, which your dog needs for fat-soluble vitamins that help with regular cell functions. Perhaps the most obvious benefit of fats and fatty acids is in your dog's coat, which will look and feel much healthier when your dog is getting the right nutrients.

There are a number of potential health issues if your dog does not get adequate fats in his daily diet.

- His coat will look less healthy.
- His skin may be dry and itchy.
- His immune system could be compromised, making it easier for your dog to get sick.
- He may have an increased risk of heart disease.

The primary concern if your dog gets too much fat is that he will gain weight and become obese, leading to additional health problems. For breeds that are predisposed to heart problems, you need to be particularly careful to ensure your dog gets the right amount of fats in his diet. An estimated 18% of Boston Terriers have heart problems.

Carbohydrates And Cooked Foods

Dogs have been living with humans for millennia, so their dietary needs have evolved like our own. They are able to eat foods with carbohydrates to supplement the energy typically provided by proteins and fats. If you cook up grains (such as barley, corn, rice, and wheat) prior to feeding them to your dog, it will be easier for your dog to digest those complex carbohydrates. This is something to keep in mind when considering what type of food you will feed your dog as you want to get a kibble (dry dog food) that uses meat instead of grains; while your dog can digest food with grains, he won't get as much of the nutritional value as he would from food that has real meat.

> **HELPFUL TIP**
> **Obesity**
>
> Many people don't understand that the Boston Terrier is supposed to be lean rather than round, meaning that many Bostons are overweight. You should be able to feel your Boston Terrier's ribs without too much effort. Obesity causes many of the same health problems in dogs as people, so if you can't feel your Boston's ribs, talk to your dog's vet about your Boston Terrier's ideal weight and how to get (and keep) that weight.

Different Dietary Requirements For Different Life Stages

Different stages of a dog's life have different nutritional needs:

- Puppies
- Adults
- Senior dogs

Puppy Food

Dog food manufacturers produce a completely different type of food for puppies for a very good reason – their nutritional needs are much different than their adult counterparts. During roughly the first 12 months of their lives, puppy's bodies are growing. To be healthy, they need more calories and have different nutritional needs to promote that growth.

Adult Dog Food

The primary difference between puppy food and adult dog food is that puppy food is higher in calories and nutrients that promote growth. Dog

CHAPTER 12   Nutrition

food producers reduce these nutrients in food made for adult dogs as they no longer need to sustain growth. As a general rule, when a dog reaches about 90% of his predicted adult size, you should switch to adult dog food.

The size of your dog is key in determining how much to feed him. The following table is a general recommendation on how much to feed your adult Boston Terrier a day. Initially, you may want to focus on the calories as you try to find the right balance for your dog.

Dog Size	Calories
10 lbs.	420 during hot months 630 during cold months
20 lbs.	700 during hot months 1,050 during cold months

Notice that most Boston Terriers don't need 1,000 calories a day most of the year. This is not a lot of food, so you need to be very aware of how many calories you are giving your dog to ensure your dog does not become overweight. This scale is for a dog's ideal weight range. If your dog is overweight or obese, ask your vet about how much you should be feeding your dog per day.

Also keep in mind that these recommendations are per day, and not per meal. Whether you feed your dog once a day or several times per day, make sure that you carefully measure out how much food you give so that you do not exceed the daily recommendation.

If you plan to add wet food, pay attention to the total calorie intake and adjust how much you feed your dog between the kibble and wet food. In other words, the total calories in the kibble and wet food should balance out so as not to exceed your dog's needs.

The same is true if you give your dog a lot of treats over the course of the day. You should factor treat calorie counts into how much you feed your dog at mealtimes.

If you plan to feed your dog homemade food, you will need to learn more about nutrition, and you will need to pay close attention to calories, and not cup measurements.

Senior Dog Food

Senior dogs aren't always capable of being as active as they were in their younger days. If you notice your dog slowing down or see that your dog isn't able to take longer walks because of joint pain or a lack of stamina, that is a good sign that your dog is entering his senior years. Consult with your vet when you think it is time to change the type of food you give your dog.

The primary difference between adult and senior dog food is that senior dog food has less fat and more antioxidants to help fight weight gain. Senior dogs also need more protein, which will probably make your dog happy because that usually means more meat and meat flavors. Protein helps to maintain your dog's aging muscles. He should be eating less phosphorous during his golden years to avoid the risk of your dog developing hyperphosphatemia. This is a condition where dogs have excessive amounts of phosphorous in their blood stream, and older dogs are at greater risk of developing it. Phosphorous is largely found in bones to help with muscle contractions and the nerves. The levels of phosphorous in the body is controlled by the kidneys. Elevated levels of phosphorous is usually an indication of a problem with the kidneys.

Senior dog food has the right number of calories for the reduced activity, so you shouldn't need to adjust how much food you give your dog, unless you notice that he is putting on weight. Consult your vet before you adjust the amount of food or if you notice that your dog is putting on weight. This could be a sign of a senior dog ailment.

Your Dog's Meal Options

You have three primary choices for what to feed your dog, or you can use a combination of the three, depending on your situation and your dog's specific needs:

- Commercial food
- Raw diet
- Homemade diet

Commercial Food

Make sure that you are buying the best dog food that you can afford. Take the time to research each of your options, particularly the nutritional value of the food, and make this an annual task. You want to make sure that the food you are giving your dog is quality food. Always account for your dog's size, energy levels, and age. Your puppy may not need puppy food as long as other breeds and dog food for seniors may not be the best option for your own senior Boston Terrier.

Pawster provides several great articles about which commercial dog foods are good for Boston Terriers. Since new foods frequently come on the market, check back occasionally to see if there are newer, better foods available. Since you have to be careful of your Boston Terrier's weight, it is well worth verifying that you are giving him the best food available.

If you aren't sure about which brand of food is best, talk with the breeder about what foods they recommend. You can ask your vet, though odds are most of them have not worked with many Boston Terriers and haven't formed an opinion yet. Breeders are really the best guides for you here, as they are experts on the breed.

Some dogs may be picky, and they can certainly get tired of having the same food repeatedly. Just as you switch up your meals, you can change what your Boston Terrier eats. While you shouldn't frequently change the brand of food, you can get foods that have different flavors. You can also change the taste by adding a bit of wet (canned) food. This is an easy change to make, giving your dog a different canned food (usually just about ¼ to 1/3 of the can for a meal, depending on your dog's size) with each meal.

For more details on commercial options, check out Dog Food Advisor. They provide reviews on the different brands, as well as providing information on recalls and contamination issues.

Commercial Dry Food

Dry dog food often comes in bags, and it is what the vast majority of people feed their dogs.

Dry Dog Food

PROS	CONS
• Convenience	• Requires research to ensure you don't buy doggie junk food
• Variety	• Packaging is not always honest
• Availability	• Recalls for food contamination
• Affordability	• Loose FDA nutritional regulations
• Manufacturers follow nutritional recommendations (not all of them follow this, so do your brand research before you buy)	• Low quality food may have questionable ingredients
• Specially formulated for different canine life stages	
• Can be used for training	
• Easy to store	

The convenience and ease on your budget means that you are almost certainly going to buy kibble for your dog. This is perfectly fine, and most dogs will be more than happy to eat kibble. Just know what brand you are currently feeding your dog, and pay attention to kibble recalls to ensure you stop feeding your dog that particular food if necessary.

Commercial Wet Food

Most dogs prefer wet dog food to kibble, but it is also more expensive. Wet dog food can be purchased in larger packs that can be very easy to store.

Wet Dog Food

PROS	CONS
• Helps keep dogs hydrated	• Dog bowls must be washed after every meal
• Has a richer scent and flavor	• Can soften bowel movements
• Easier to eat for dogs with dental problems (particularly those missing teeth) or if a dog has been ill	• Can be messier than kibble
	• Once opened, it has a very short shelf life, and should be covered and refrigerated
• Convenient and easy to serve	• More expensive than dry dog food, and comes in small quantities
• Unopened, it can last between 1 and 3 years	
• Balanced based on current pet nutrition recommendations	• Packaging is not always honest
	• Recalls for food contamination
	• Loose FDA regulations

Like dry dog food, wet dog food is convenient, and picky dogs are much more likely to eat it than kibble. When your dog gets sick, it is best to use wet dog food to ensure that he is eating so that he gets the necessary nutrition he needs each day. It may be a bit harder to switch back to kibble once he is healthy, but you can always continue to add a little wet food to make each meal more appetizing to your dog.

Raw Diet

For dogs like the Boston Terrier that have food allergies, raw diets can help to keep your dog from having an allergic reaction to wheat and processed foods. Raw diets are heavy in raw meats, bones, vegetables, and specific supplements. Some of the benefits to a raw diet include:

• Improves your dog's coat and skin

CHAPTER 12   Nutrition

- Improves immune system
- Improves health (as a result of better digestion)
- Increases energy
- Increases muscle mass

Raw diets are meant to give your dog the kind of food he ate before being domesticated. It means giving your dog uncooked meats, whole (uncooked) bones, and a bit of dairy products. It doesn't include any processed food of any kind – not even food cooked in your kitchen.

There are potential risks to this diet. Dogs have been domesticated for millennia, and their digestive system has evolved as they have. Trying to force them back on the kind of diet they used to eat does not always work as intended because they may not be able to fully digest it anymore. There are also a lot of risks with feeding dogs uncooked meals, particularly if the food has been contaminated. Things like bacteria pose a serious risk and can be transferred to you if your dog gets sick. Many medical professionals also warn about the dangers of giving dogs bones, even if they are uncooked. Bones can splinter in your dog's mouth, puncturing the esophagus or stomach.

The Canine Journal provides a lot of information about the raw diet, including how to transition your current dog to this diet and different recipes for your dog.

Homemade Diet

If you regularly make your own food (from scratch, not with a microwave or boxed meal), it really doesn't take that much more time to provide an equally healthy meal for your companion.

Keeping in mind the foods that your Boston Terrier absolutely should not eat, you can mix some of the food you make for yourself into your Boston Terrier's meal. Just make sure to add a bit more of what your Boston Terrier needs to the puppy's food bowl. Although you and your Boston Terrier have distinctly different dietary needs, you can tailor your foods to include nutrients that your dog needs.

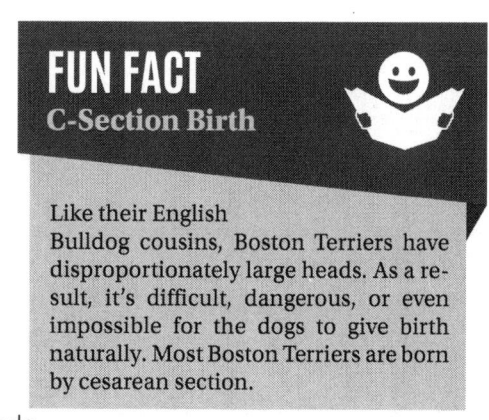

> **FUN FACT**
> **C-Section Birth**
>
> Like their English Bulldog cousins, Boston Terriers have disproportionately large heads. As a result, it's difficult, dangerous, or even impossible for the dogs to give birth naturally. Most Boston Terriers are born by cesarean section.

Photo Courtesy of Allyson Vokaty

Do not feed your Boston Terrier from your plate. Split the food, placing your dog's meal into a bowl so that your canine understands that your food is just for you. The best home cooked meals should be planned in advance so that your Boston Terrier is getting the right nutritional balance.

Typically, 50% of your dog's food should be animal protein (fish, poultry, and organ meats). About 25% should be full of complex carbohydrates. The remaining 25% should be from fruits and vegetables, particularly foods like pumpkin, apples, bananas, and green beans. These foods provide additional flavor that your Boston Terrier will probably love while making him feel full faster, so that the chance of overeating is reduced.

The following are a few sites you can use to learn to make meals for canines. Some of them are not Boston Terrier specific, so if you have more than one dog, these meals can be made for all of your furry canine friends:

- Anipetkingdom.com
- Boston Terrier Secrets
- Dogsaholic
- Life with Dogs

Scheduling Meals

Your Boston Terrier will likely expect you to stick to a schedule, and that definitely includes mealtimes. This is a breed that will have no problem with letting you know you are late with the food. If treats and snacks are something you establish as normal early on, your dog will believe that treats are also a part of the routine and will expect them.

Food Allergies And Intolerance

"Variety is the key to a balanced diet, just as it is with our own diets. If feeding kibble, a rotation of flavors (protein sources) every 2 or 3 bags would be ideal. Getting a puppy used to variety when young will make for an easier adult dog to live with as far as being more open minded to different foods and not as prone to dietary intolerances from food changes."

Maxine Uzoff
Oui Bostons

Whenever you start your dog on a new type of dog food (even if it is the same brand that your dog is accustomed to, but a different flavor), you need to monitor him as he becomes accustomed to it. Food allergies are fairly common, so you will need to be aware of the symptoms of food allergies. Food allergies in dogs tend to manifest themselves as hot spots, which are similar to rashes in humans. Your dog may start scratching or chewing specific spots on his body. His fur could start falling out around those spots.

Some dogs don't have a single hot spot, but the allergy shows up on their entire coat. If your Boston Terrier seems to be shedding more fur than normal, take your dog to the vet to have him checked for food allergies.

Sticking to a grain-free diet can help ensure that your Boston Terrier is getting the right nutrition without suffering food intolerance. If you do give your dog something that his stomach cannot handle, it will probably be obvious when your dog is unable to hold his bowels. If he is already housetrained, he will probably either pant at you or whimper to let you know that he needs to go outside. Don't ignore either of these pleas. Get him outside as quickly as you can so that he does not have an accident. Flatulence will probably occur more often if your Boston Terrier has a food intolerance.

Since the symptoms of food allergies and tolerances can be similar to a dog's reaction to nutritional deficiencies (particularly a lack of fats in a dog's diet), you should visit your vet if you notice any problems with your dog's coat or skin.

CHAPTER 13
An Entertainer Who Is Game For Fun Around The Home

Boston Terriers are an absolute delight to have around the home. Their natural enthusiasm and positive outlook make them fantastic companions that will love playing with you when you are available. They will watch you glumly for any sign that you are able to play all of the time. Then once you acknowledge your little Boston Terrier, all bets are off because that is the sign that it is time to do a bit of play or head out for a walk.

Remember, don't take your Boston Terrier out during the heat of the day most of the year. Their short snouts make it easy for them to overheat and die. During the summer, take them out in the early morning or around sundown to ensure they stay cool enough for the walk.

Photo Courtesy of Katherine Garcia

CHAPTER 13   An Entertainer Who Is Game For Fun Around The Home

Photo Courtesy of Allyson Vokaty

Exercise Needs

"A daily short walk is ideal. But if you cannot walk with your Boston regularly just playing fetch is a great excersize for them. If you have a fenced yard they can run around freely also and run out some of that Boston energy! Keep in mind that they are brachisephalic, which also means that they cannot be put in certain situations where they will overheat, so please don't expect your Boston to go on long summer hikes with the family. They will be much happier and safer, if left home for a few hours."

Markella Motz
Bly Mountain Bostons

Bringing a Boston Terrier into your home means you are agreeing to daily exercise, even when he is still a puppy. Dogs don't want to misbehave, but if they are bored, mischief is inevitable. Fortunately, their size

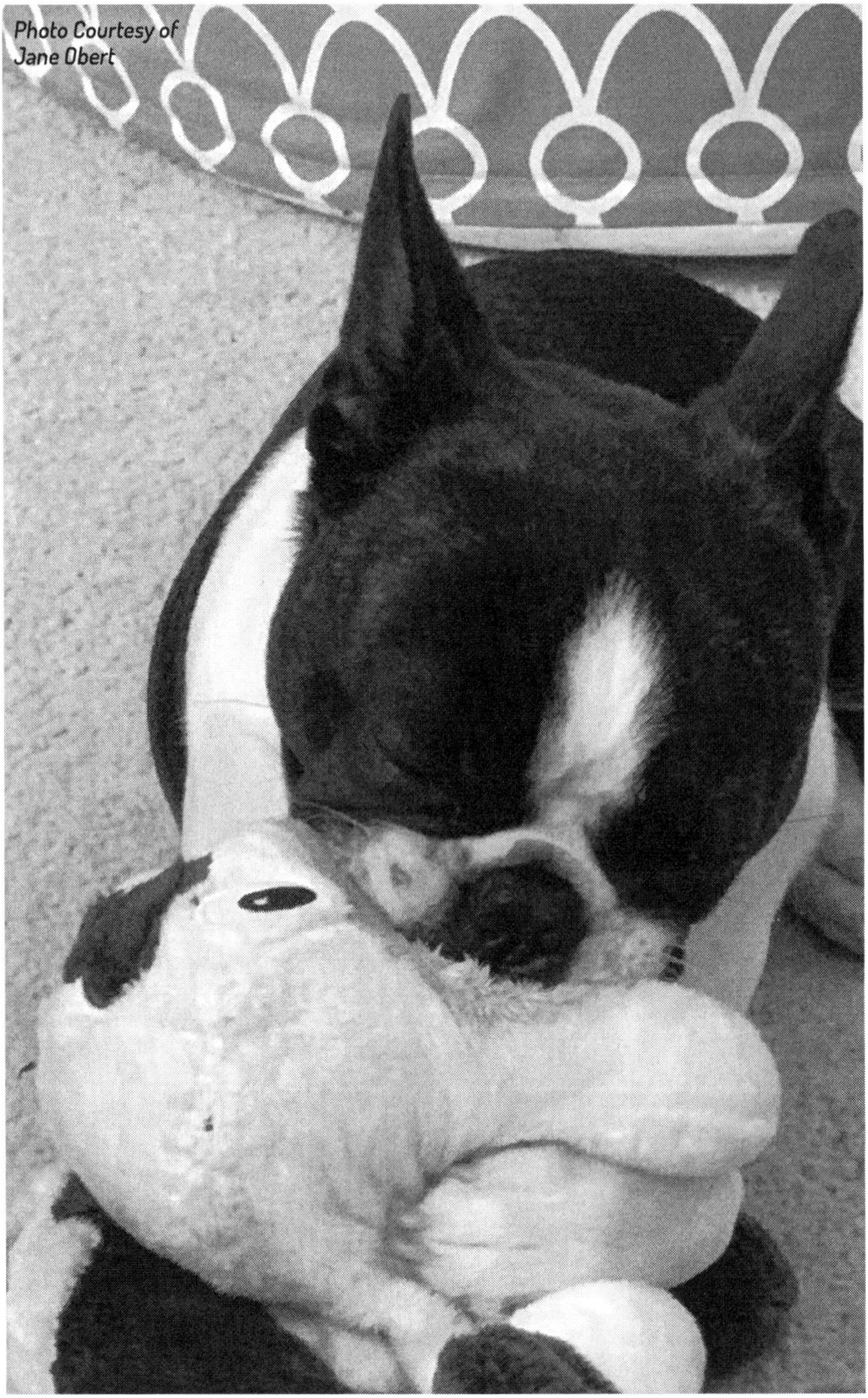
Photo Courtesy of Jane Obert

CHAPTER 13   An Entertainer Who Is Game For Fun Around The Home

makes exercising enough pretty easy, so when you finally leave your dog home alone, it's unlikely that your furniture or other things will be shredded in your absence.

Since weight problems are directly related to a lack of exercise, if your dog is gaining weight, that could be a sign that he isn't getting enough time moving about. Fortunately, it's easy to correct that. You have a lot of options for how to make sure your dog gets enough of a workout – it is much easier (and healthier for your friend) to do more with your dog than to just measure calories.

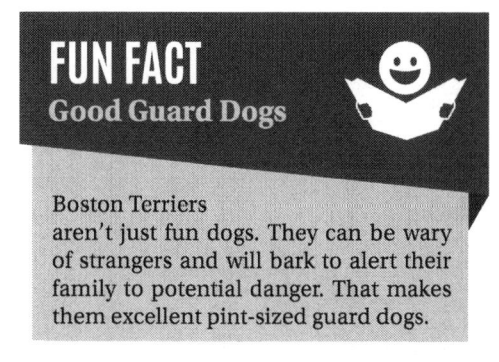

> **FUN FACT**
> **Good Guard Dogs**
>
> Boston Terriers aren't just fun dogs. They can be wary of strangers and will bark to alert their family to potential danger. That makes them excellent pint-sized guard dogs.

A Wide, Easy Activity Range

Their appearance and inquisitive personality makes Boston Terriers a popular breed. They love to explore new areas, but you need to be careful about the time of day, especially in summer. Still, the more different activities that you do with your dog, the happier you will both be. Just remember to take water and not let your dog get too hot.

Fetch

Most dogs love this game, but Boston Terriers can get very enthusiastic about chasing down something you throw because of the very excited response you have when they return with it. The interaction is fun and chasing after the ball is perfect for tiring out your dog. They are also inclined to chase and return stuff to you because they are terriers.

You may want to keep it to an outdoor activity, especially if you have kids, so that things around your home don't get broken. If so, you can never slip up and allow fetch on a rainy day because that will teach your Boston Terrier that you can be convinced to give in with the right tactics.

In The Sprinkler

As a brachial dog, Boston Terriers tend to overheat in the hot months. If you want to go outside, especially with kids, bust out the sprinklers so everyone can have a good time. As your kids run through it, your Boston Terrier will try to catch the water. This is the perfect way to get everyone outside for some fun without having to worry as much about your pup getting too hot. You still shouldn't stay out too long, as much because of sunburns as overheating. A good 20 or 30 minutes should be more than enough to tire everyone out and give you a bit of peace when they return to the indoors.

Agility Training

Better known as obstacle courses, agility training is a great way to keep your adult dog running and happy. You get to guide your dog through the course, helping not only to build your bond, but also to give your dog a chance to feel more comfortable when he is outside the home, or at least learn that he doesn't need to try to dominate everyone in the area. Since you are the one in control, and your dog will likely be confused in the beginning, be prepared to look a bit silly at first. The point is to have fun and to keep your dog engaged, so getting and keeping his attention is key to being successful.

Two to three hours of dedicated time are recommended a week, with one of those hours going to a weekly class. The more you can train at home, the better your dog will do in this sport.

Photo Courtesy of Jen Buck

Playtime! And More Playtime!

Just because there is inclement weather doesn't mean that your dog's energy levels will be any lower, or that boredom won't set in, so you'll need to plan to keep your dog's exercise schedule consistent, even when you are stuck inside the house. Of course, if you can put your dog out to play in the snow in a backyard, that will be fantastic as he can tire himself out in his excitement. During rain and heat, you need to find the right activities to tire your canine without going outside for extended periods of time. Here are some alternatives to help expend your Boston Terrier's energy.

CHAPTER 13   An Entertainer Who Is Game For Fun Around The Home

1. Let your Boston Terrier chase a laser pointer. This works for some Boston Terriers, but not all. If your dog seems interested, this can keep him happily occupied for as long as you want to play or until he gets bored.

2. Hide and seek is a game you can play once your dog knows about proper behavior in the home, whether you have him find you or a favorite toy you've hidden.

3. Puzzle toys are a great way to get your dog to move around without you having to do much. Many of the games come with treats, and knowing Boston Terriers, it won't be long before your dog figures out how to get the food out of the toy, so make sure you rotate various puzzles at playtime. Use these kinds of toys sparingly to avoid piling on the extra calories.

4. Treat hunting is something that you can do easily inside and that will be very exciting for your dog. Your dog will have time for something to help get rid of the energy while engaging that clever little brain. Just show your pup that you have a treat, then let him watch you hide it. Of course, he will find it quickly and you should lavish the praise for this. After a couple of times, have someone distract your pup as you hide the treat you just showed him. This helps your Boston Terrier to learn the point of the game, and it will probably become a favorite.

Photo Courtesy of Julie Carelock

CHAPTER 14
Grooming – Productive Bonding

Boston Terriers are great dogs to have for many reasons, and ease of grooming is one of them. With their short hair and small frame, grooming Boston Terriers is extremely easy. That said, they should be kept clean, and you will need to be careful of your Boston Terrier's eyes and ears. Since they have allergies, it is common for Boston Terriers to have problems with their coats. Regular grooming will help you to detect a potential problem early on.

This chapter provides a baseline for making sure your Boston Terrier's coat is clean and healthy, but feel free to look online and elsewhere for additional ways to make the coat really shine if you have the time to do some additional care.

Grooming Tools

You don't need too many tools to properly groom your Boston Terrier. Make sure you have the following items on hand before your puppy or adult dog arrives:

- A bristle or pin brush for his coat; you can also get a rubber palm brush or mitt to make the experience more like petting.
- Shampoo (check Barkspace and Pet Reviews for the latest recommendations for a breed with potential skin conditions) – use mild shampoo specifically for dogs
- Nail trimmers
- Toothbrush and toothpaste (check the American Kennel Club for the latest recommendations) – use toothpaste made specifically for dogs.

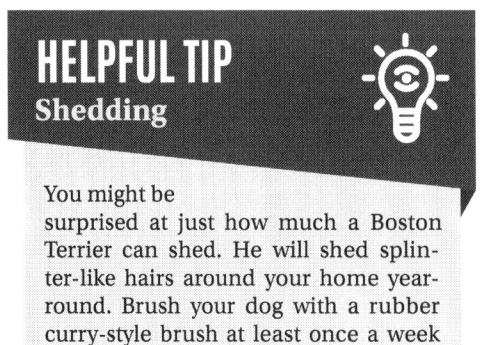

> **HELPFUL TIP**
> **Shedding**
>
> You might be surprised at just how much a Boston Terrier can shed. He will shed splinter-like hairs around your home year-round. Brush your dog with a rubber curry-style brush at least once a week to help remove hair before it ends up on your furniture. A high-quality food should help reduce shedding compared to a cheap one full of filler ingredients.

Coat Management

Boston Terriers are not prolific shedders, but a weekly brushing will make sure that you don't have much fur flying around your home. Starting a grooming routine when your puppy is young will be a great bonding experience for both you and your newest family member. It is also a good time to start teaching your puppy to listen to you.

> **FUN FACT**
> **Famous Owners**
>
> Many famous people have owned Boston Terriers over the years, including musician Louis Armstrong and reality show host Alison Sweeney. Rose McGowan is such a big fan of Bostons that she has owned three, and she also works with a Boston Terrier rescue to provide a better life for dogs who are surrendered.

Puppies

When they are puppies, Boston Terriers are easy to manage. Daily brushing not only can reduce how much your puppy sheds, but it helps you to build a bond with the dog. Yes, it will be a bit challenging in the beginning because puppies don't sit still for long periods of time. There will be a lot of wiggling and attempts to play. Trying to tell your puppy that the brush is not a toy clearly isn't going to work, so be prepared to be patient during each brushing session.

On the other hand, your pup will be so adorable, you probably won't mind that grooming takes a bit longer. Just make sure you let your pup know that this is a serious effort and playing comes after grooming. Otherwise, your Boston Terrier is going to always try to play, which will make brushing him more time consuming. Plan to brush your puppy after a vigorous exercise session so that your Boston Terrier has far less energy to fight or play.

Adult Dogs

Brushing weekly is recommended to keep loose hairs to a minimum. If you properly train your puppy how to behave, brushing him will be easy when he is an adult. If not, it may prove to be a little challenging unless you make sure your dog is tired first.

If you rescued an adult Boston Terrier, it may take a little while to get the dog used to being brushed frequently. If you aren't able to get your dog to feel comfortable with the brushing in the beginning, you can work it into your schedule, like training.

Senior Dogs

You can continue to brush your old friend once a week, or you can brush him more often if you would like. Grooming sessions are a good way to check for issues while giving your older pup a nice massage to ease any pain, as well as being a great way of having dedicated time together. While brushing your dog, look for any changes to the skin, such as bumps or fatty lumps. These may need to be mentioned to the vet during a regular visit if the bumps or lumps are very large.

Allergies

If your Boston Terrier is suffering from hot spots or if you notice his coat thinning out during grooming sessions, watch for these other problems, which could be a sign of allergies:

- Wounds take longer to heal
- Weak immune system
- Aching joints
- Hair is falling out
- Ear infections

Regular brushing ensures that you are more aware of the state of your Boston Terrier's coat, which can help you more quickly identify when your little dear is suffering from allergies. If you notice these issues, take your Boston Terrier to the vet.

Bath Time

"Do not over bathe your Boston Terrier. This can dry their skin out and cause skin issues. Once a month is adequate in most cases. Use baby wipes between baths to clean their feet, face, and butt when needed."

Linda Reaves
Bama's Hurricane Creek Kennel

With short coats, baths are not required very often. Most professionals recommend a bath when your Boston Terrier starts to smell or has gotten dirty. Since they have allergies and more sensitive skin, you don't want to wash them too often (unless your Boston Terrier has a penchant for getting

CHAPTER 14   Grooming – Productive Bonding

dirty or rolling in smelly things – like garbage). Washing your dog too often can make his skin itchy and dry, which can lead to sores and other problems as your poor pup tries to relieve the itching.

Of course, if your Boston Terrier gets dirty (which may happen whenever you go out exploring or hiking), then you'll need to take the time to bathe your canine after each of these events. Make sure the water isn't too cold or too hot, but comfortably warm. Make sure you don't get his head wet. Washing his face is covered in the next section.

STEPS FOR BATH TIME

1. GET EVERYTHING YOU WILL NEED IN ONE PLACE
Make sure you have the following supplies ready: shampoo and conditioner (made for dogs), one large cup, towels, brush, non-slip tub mat.

2. TAKE YOUR BOSTON TERRIER OUT FOR A WALK.
This will both tire your dog and make him a little hotter, which will make the bath less hated – maybe even appreciated.

3. RUN THE WATER
Make sure that the temperature is lukewarm but not hot, especially if you have just finished a walk. If you are washing him in a bathtub, you only need enough water to cover up to your pup's stomach.

4. TALK IN A STRONG CONFIDENT VOICE
Don't use baby talk. Your Boston Terrier needs a confident leader, not to be treated like an infant.

5. PLACE THE DOG IN THE TUB
and use the cup to wash the dog. Don't use too much soap – it isn't necessary. You can fully soak the dog starting at the neck and going to the rump. It is fine to get him wet all at once, then to suds him up, or you can do it a bit at a time if your dog is very wiggly. Just make sure that you don't get any water on his head.

6. TALK TO YOUR DOG
while you are bathing him, keeping in mind you need to talk with confidence, not a high tone.

7. MAKE SURE YOU DON'T GET WATER IN YOUR DOG'S EYES OR EARS
You don't need to get water on the top of your dog's head. Use a wet hand and gently scrub around his eyes and ears, being careful to avoid getting soap or water in either.

8. RINSE OFF AGAINST THE GRAIN
Make sure rinse the water up against the natural lay of the fur so that there isn't any shampoo left beneath the hairs.

9. TOWEL DRY AND BRUSH
Toweling drying and rushing are great bonding times, towel dry and then brush gently so your Boston enjoys the process and is excited for the next bath!

CHAPTER 14   Grooming – Productive Bonding

You can use these practices with other kinds of bathing, such as outside or at a public washing facility, modifying them to the tools you have at hand.

The first few times you bathe your dog, pay attention to the things that bother or scare him. If he is afraid of running water, make sure you don't have the water running when your dog is in the tub. If he moves a lot when you start to apply the shampoo, it could indicate the smell is too strong. You need to modify the process to make it as comfortable for your dog as possible.

Keep in mind that you have to be patient and calm during the bath. If you get upset or take out your frustration on your dog, it will make all future baths that much more difficult as your dog will begin to stop trusting you. This isn't a fight for dominance, it is an honest lack of understanding for why you are torturing your dog when he already does so much to clean himself (from his standpoint). Keep a calm, loving tone as you wash your dog to make it a little easier next time. Sure, your Boston Terrier may scream, throw a tantrum, or wiggle excessively, but the better you take it, the more the dog will learn that bathing is simply a part of being in the pack.

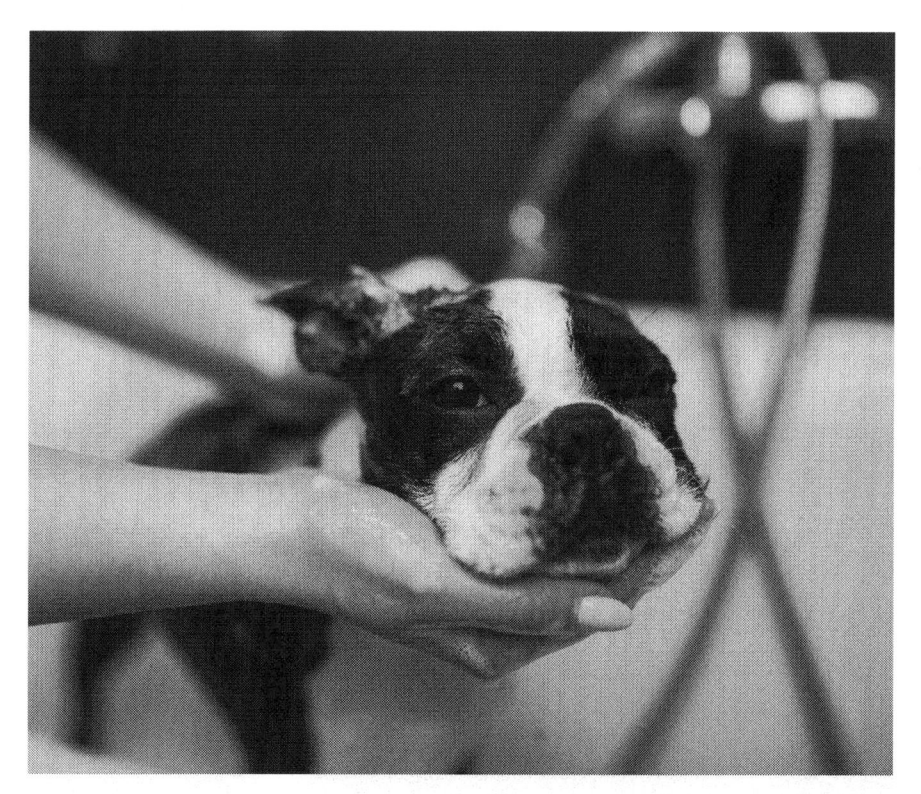

Cleaning Eyes And Ears

"Don't forget to wipe out ears on occasional bath days with a dab of isopropal alcohol on a piece of a cotton ball. This will ensure your Boston's ears will stay shiny and clean."

Maxine Uzoff
Oui Bostons

Use a washcloth to wash your dog's face. You will need to get in the folds of his skin. This should be done daily so that his eyes and skin don't get irritated from dirt that could remain in the folds of his facial skin.

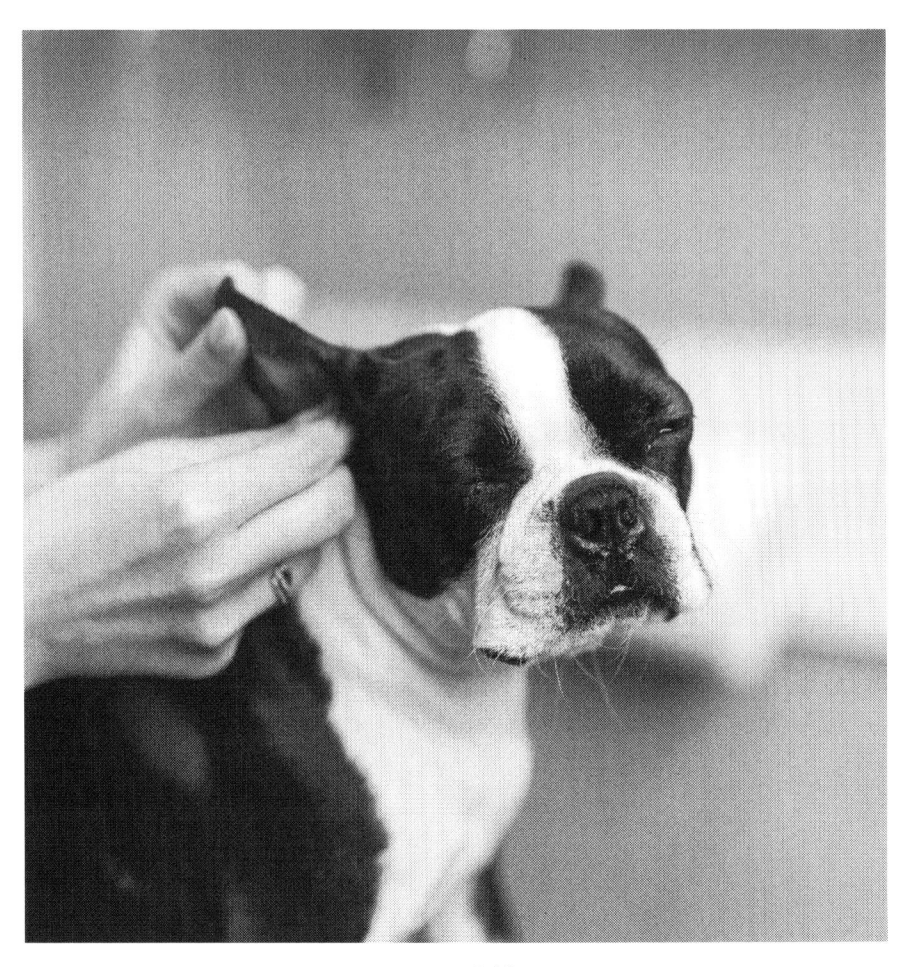

When you bathe your Boston Terrier, be careful not to get water in his ears. You should also make a habit of checking his ears once a week to make sure they're healthy. He may have allergies that make the inside of his ears look red. A warm, moist pad can be used on the surface part of the ear. If the redness doesn't look better in a day, make an appointment to visit the vet. If you see wax buildup, you can very gently wipe it away. Never put anything in your dog's ears.

Boston Terriers have several genetic eye conditions (Chapter 16), so take the time to always check your dog's eyes while you are grooming him. Cataracts are a fairly common problem for all dogs as they age. If you see cloudy eyes, have your Boston Terrier checked. If he's developing cataracts, you may need to take the pup in to have them removed because cataracts can lead to blindness.

Trimming Nails

"Keep your Boston's toenails Dremeled every 1-4 weeks or the nails tend to overgrow and can cause arthritis in their feet later in life if nails are continually are left overgrown. Keeping nails Dremeled regularly as a young puppy will make nail care immeasurably easier than if attempting to begin later in life. Many dogs are particular about having their front feet handled anyway so this is a simple but important point to get puppies used to the Dremel 'tickle' when young."

Maxine Uzoff
Oui Bostons

Cutting a Boston Terrier's nails can difficult because some have black nails or it can be difficult to tell how much is too much, which means that you may cut too much off and cause the quick to bleed. It's best to have an expert cut your dog's nails until you can see how it's done. If you have not cut a dog's nails before, you need to learn from a professional as the nails can bleed a lot if done wrong. Since it can be difficult to tell how far to go while trimming a Boston Terrier's nails, you need to learn from an expert before you try it yourself. If you already know how to cut a dog's nails, make sure to have some styptic powder nearby in case you cut too much off.

To know when your pup needs his nails cut, pay attention when your dog is walking on hard surfaces to make sure his nails aren't clicking. If they are, then you should increase how often you get your dog's nails trimmed. As a general rule, once a month is recommended.

Oral Health And Brushing Your Dog's Teeth

Boston Terriers need their teeth brushed daily to reduce dental problems as they tend to have problems with their teeth and gums. You probably will want to learn to do it yourself over having to visit a shop once a week. It's also nice to know how to brush your dog's teeth if his breath smells bad or he eats something that smells foul.

Again, you have to learn to be patient and keep it from being an all-out fight with your dog. It is a little weird, and your Boston Terrier may not be terribly happy with someone putting stuff in his mouth. However, once he is accustomed to it, the task will likely only take a few minutes a day.

Always use a toothpaste that is made for dogs. Human toothpaste can be toxic to dogs. The flavor of dog toothpaste will also make it easier to brush your dog's teeth – or at least entertaining as he tries to eat it. To start brushing your pup's teeth:Once your dog seems all right with you brushing his teeth with your finger, try the same steps with a canine toothbrush. It may be a similar song and dance in the beginning, but it shouldn't take nearly as long for him to accept the toothbrush. It could take a couple of weeks before you can graduate to a toothbrush, but even if it does take that long, it's still great bonding time.

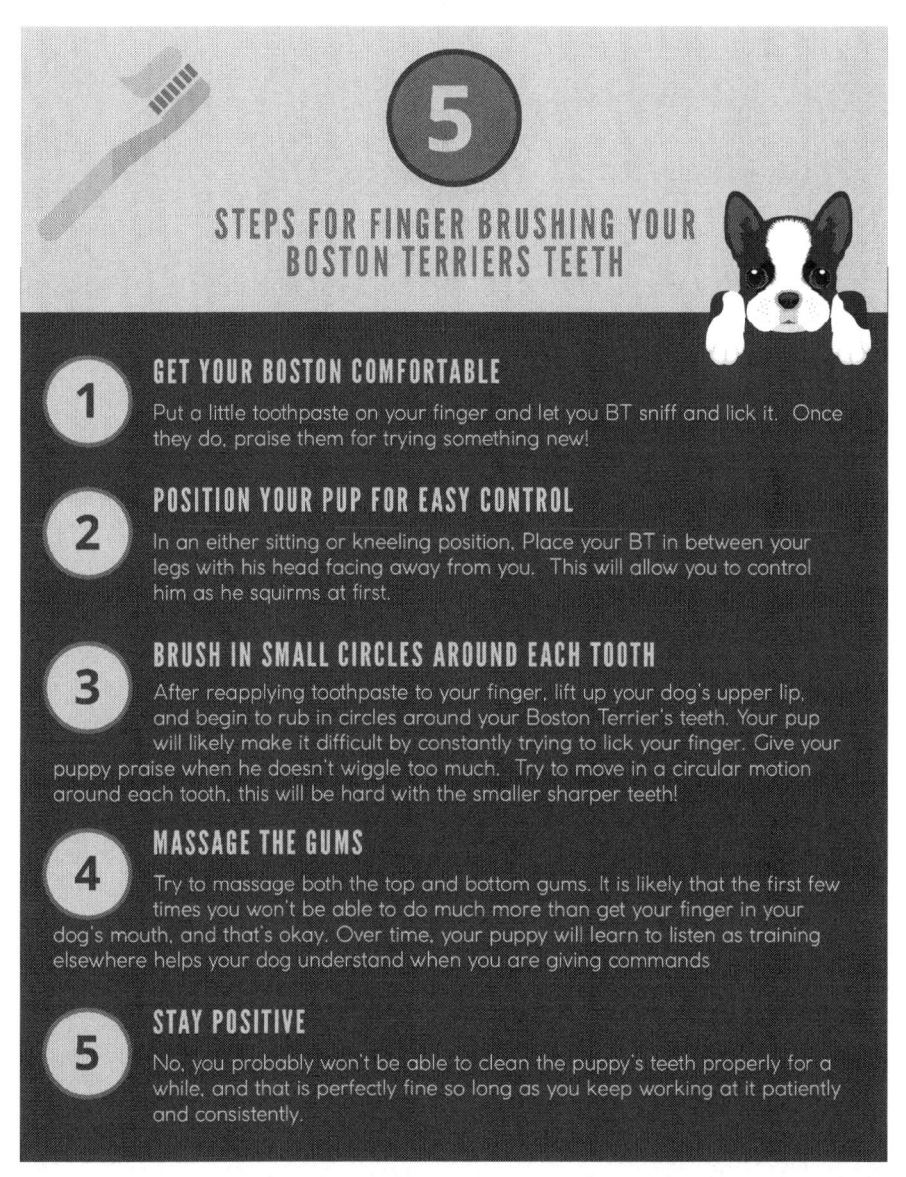

CHAPTER 14   Grooming – Productive Bonding

5 STEPS FOR FINGER BRUSHING YOUR BOSTON TERRIERS TEETH

1. GET YOUR BOSTON COMFORTABLE

Put a little toothpaste on your finger and let you BT sniff and lick it. Once they do, praise them for trying something new!

2. POSITION YOUR PUP FOR EASY CONTROL

In an either sitting or kneeling position. Place your BT in between your legs with his head facing away from you. This will allow you to control him as he squirms at first.

3. BRUSH IN SMALL CIRCLES AROUND EACH TOOTH

After reapplying toothpaste to your finger, lift up your dog's upper lip, and begin to rub in circles around your Boston Terrier's teeth. Your pup will likely make it difficult by constantly trying to lick your finger. Give your puppy praise when he doesn't wiggle too much. Try to move in a circular motion around each tooth, this will be hard with the smaller sharper teeth!

4. MASSAGE THE GUMS

Try to massage both the top and bottom gums. It is likely that the first few times you won't be able to do much more than get your finger in your dog's mouth, and that's okay. Over time, your puppy will learn to listen as training elsewhere helps your dog understand when you are giving commands

5. STAY POSITIVE

No, you probably won't be able to clean the puppy's teeth properly for a while, and that is perfectly fine so long as you keep working at it patiently and consistently.

Once your dog seems all right with you brushing his teeth with your finger, try the same steps with a canine toothbrush. It may be a similar song and dance in the beginning, but it shouldn't take nearly as long for him to accept the toothbrush. It could take a couple of weeks before you can graduate to a toothbrush, but even if it does take that long, it's still great bonding time.

CHAPTER 15
General Health Issues: Allergies, Parasites, And Vaccinations

Environmental factors largely determine whether or not your dog gets parasites. For example, if you live near a wooded area, your dog is at a greater risk of ticks than a dog that lives in the city. Talk to your vet about particular environmental risks to your dog. Given that Boston Terriers have a greater chance of allergies and may have sensitive skin, you will want to keep an eye on your Boston Terrier's fur after he has been outside.

The Role Of Your Veterinarian

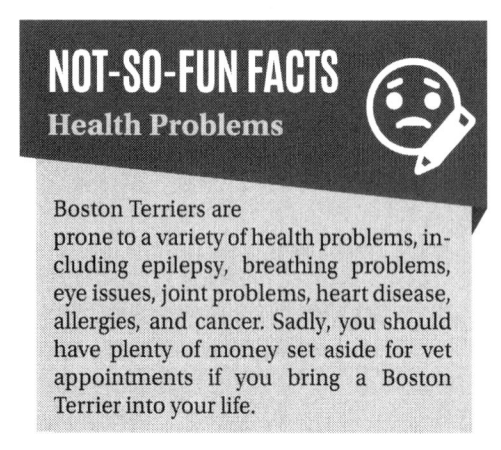

> **NOT-SO-FUN FACTS**
> **Health Problems**
>
> Boston Terriers are prone to a variety of health problems, including epilepsy, breathing problems, eye issues, joint problems, heart disease, allergies, and cancer. Sadly, you should have plenty of money set aside for vet appointments if you bring a Boston Terrier into your life.

From getting annual vaccines updated to health checkups, regularly scheduled vet visits will make sure that your Boston Terrier stays healthy. If your Boston Terrier seems sluggish or less excited than usual, it could be a sign that there is something wrong with him. Fortunately, the breed's outgoing personality tends to make it easy to tell when they aren't feeling well. Annual visits to the vet will ensure there isn't a problem that is slowly draining the energy or health from your dog.

Health checkups also make sure that your Boston Terrier is aging well. If there are any early symptoms of something potentially wrong with your dog over the years (such as arthritis), an early diagnosis will allow you to start making adjustments early. The vet can help you come up with ways to manage pain and problems that come with the aging process and will be able to recommend adjustments to the schedule to accommodate your canine's aging body and diminishing abilities. This will ensure that you can keep having fun together without hurting your dog.

Vets can provide treatments and/or preventive medications for the different parasites and microscopic threats that your dog may encounter when he is outside, during interactions with other dogs, or from exposure to animals outside your home.

Allergies

Like people, dogs can have allergies, and Boston Terriers are often affected by this problem. They usually don't have the same kind of reaction as people though. Instead of sneezing, coughing, and runny noses, allergies often present as skin irritations. The scientific name for environmental allergies is atopic dermatitis, but it's more difficult to tell whether the problem is with the environment or the food you're giving your dog. The symptoms tend to be similar in dogs for both types of allergies:

- Itching/scratching, particularly around the face
- Hot spots
- Ear infections
- Skin infections
- Runny eyes and nose (not as common)

Grooming your dog is a great time to pay attention to many of these potential problems.

Dogs often develop allergies when they are between 1 and 5 years old. Once they develop an allergy, canines don't outgrow the problem. Usually dog allergies are related to skin exposure, but some canines can be allergic to inhaling microscopic particles, such as dust, molds, and pollens.

Since the symptoms are the same for food and environmental allergies, you will need to talk to your vet about determining the cause. If your dog has a food allergy, all you have to do is change the food that you give him. If he has an environmental allergy, he will need medication, just as humans do. Because of this, you will want to know if the problem is from something seasonal (like pollen) or something year round so you will know when to treat your dog.

As with humans, completely eliminating the problem really isn't reasonable – there is only so much you can do to change the environment around your dog. There are several types of medications that can help your dog become less sensitive to the allergens.

Photo Courtesy of Laura Heyne

- Antibacterials/Antifungals – Shampoos, pills, and creams usually do not treat the allergy but the problems that come with allergies, such as bacterial and yeast infections.

- Anti-inflammatories – These are over-the-counter oral medications that are comparable to allergy medicine for people. You will need to be careful if you use these medications, monitoring your dog to see if he has any adverse effects. Don't start to give your dog any medication without first consulting with the vet. If your dog has a bad reaction, such as lethargy, diarrhea, or dehydration you should consult with your vet.

- Immunotherapy – A series of shots can help reduce your dog's sensitivity to whatever he is allergic to. This is something you can do at home, so you won't need to take your dog to the vet to complete the series. Learn how to give the shots from your vet, and then you can find out how to get the shots for your area. Scientists are also developing an oral version of the medication to make it easier to take care of your dog.

- Topical – This medication tends to be a type of shampoo and conditioner that will remove any allergens from your dog's fur. Giving your dog a warm (not hot) bath can also help relieve itching.

Talk with your vet about the medications that are available for your dog to determine the best treatment for your situation and your Boston Terrier's needs.

Inhalant And Environmental Allergies

Inhalant allergies are caused by things like dust, pollen, mold, and even dog dander. A dog's reaction tends to be different than a person's reaction. Instead of sneezing and having a runny nose, dogs tend to itch more because of the allergy. Your dog might scratch at a particular hot spot or he might start to paw at his eyes and ears. Some dogs do have runny noses and sneeze prolifically, but this is usually in addition to scratching.

Contact Allergies

Contact allergies mean that your dog has touched something that triggers an allergic reaction. Things like wool, chemicals in a flea treatment, and certain grasses can trigger irritation in a dog's skin, even causing discoloration. If left untreated, the allergic reaction can begin emitting strong odors and cause fur loss.

Like food allergies, contact allergies are easy to treat because once you know what is irritating your dog's skin, you can remove the problem.

Photo Courtesy of Tabitha Lynn

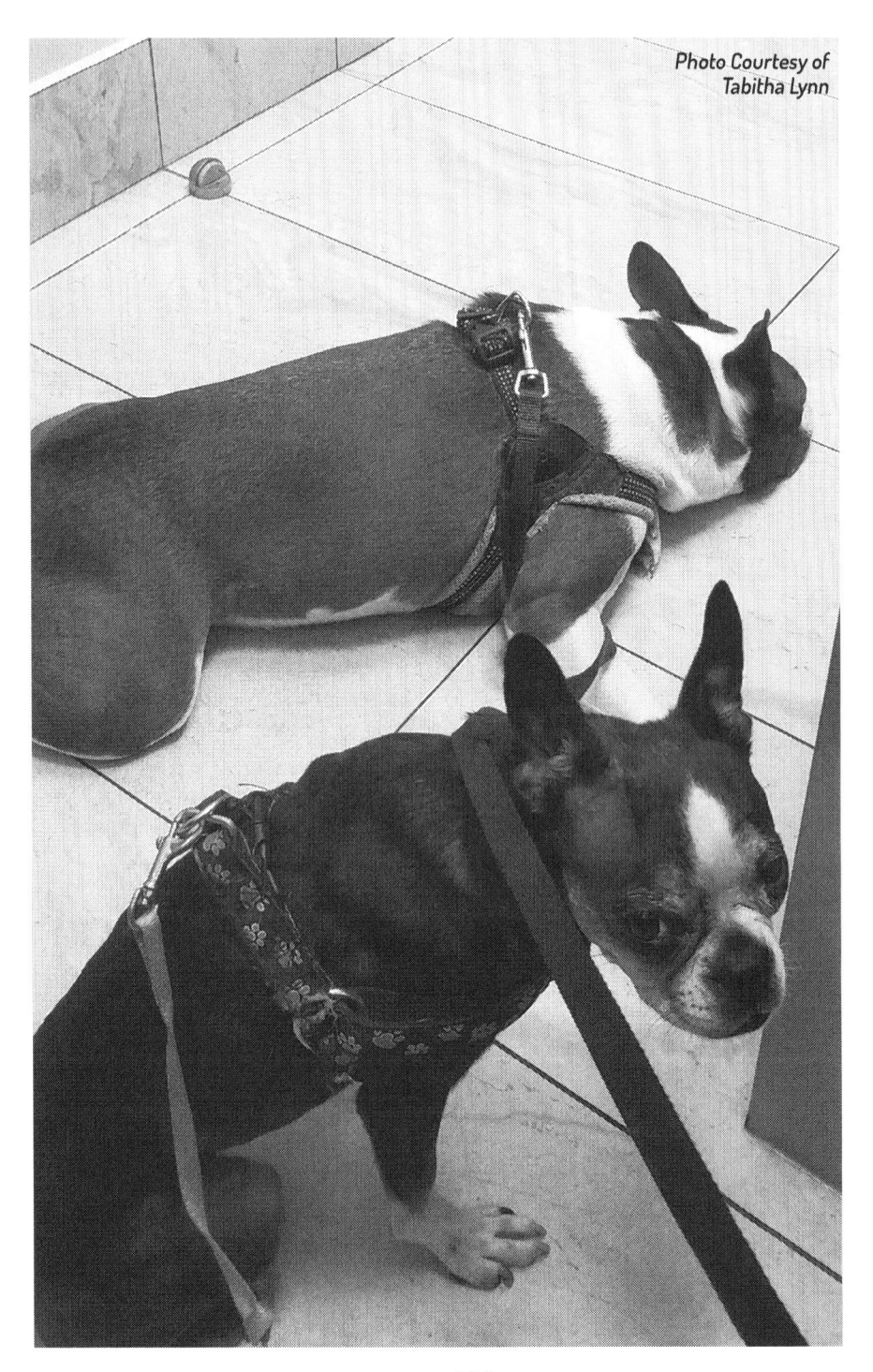

CHAPTER 15   General Health Issues: Allergies, Parasites, And Vaccinations

Fleas And Ticks

Boston Terriers tend to love being wherever you are, so if you love to be outside, you will need to be very careful about fleas and ticks. Even in your backyard, fleas are a problem nearly year round. Neither parasite is easy to see because parts of the Boston Terrier's coat are black. Therefore, you can't allow any lapse in anti-flea and tick treatment, even in the winter.

Make it a habit to check for ticks after every outing into the woods, or near long grass or wild plants. Comb through your dog's fur and check his skin for irritation and parasites. Since you will be doing this often, you should be able to notice when there's a change, such as a new bump, for example. Since your dog will be very happy to spend time with you, the skin check shouldn't take long.

Fleas are problematic because they're far more mobile than ticks. The best way to look for fleas is to make it a regular part of your brushing sessions. You can also look for behavioral indicators, such as incessant scratching and licking. You will need to use flea preventative products on a regular basis once your puppy reaches an appropriate age.

Along with being annoying, both can carry parasites and illnesses that can be passed on to you and your dog. Ticks notoriously carry Lyme disease, which can be debilitating or deadly if untreated. Lyme disease symptoms include headaches, fever, and fatigue. The bit itself often has a red circle around it that may grow. Since your dog will likely start to act sluggish after you find a tick attached to his skin, make sure to look for the circular rash, and if you see one or aren't sure, go to the vet to have it checked.

The FDA has issued a warning about some store bought treatments. Whether you look into purchasing treatments that have to be applied monthly or a collar for constant protection, you need to check the treatment to see if it contains isoxazoline (included in Bravecto, Nexgard, Credelio, and Simparica) because this ingredient can have an adverse effect on pets. While other ingredients are safe for pets when used in the proper doses, if you use a product that is meant for a larger dog, it can be toxic to your dog. Consult with your vet about recommended treatments to ensure that you get the right dose of flea and tick repellant for your dog's size and needs. When you start applying the treatment, monitor your dog for the following issues:

- Diarrhea/vomiting
- Trembling

Vanessa RICHIE | The Complete Guide to Boston Terriers

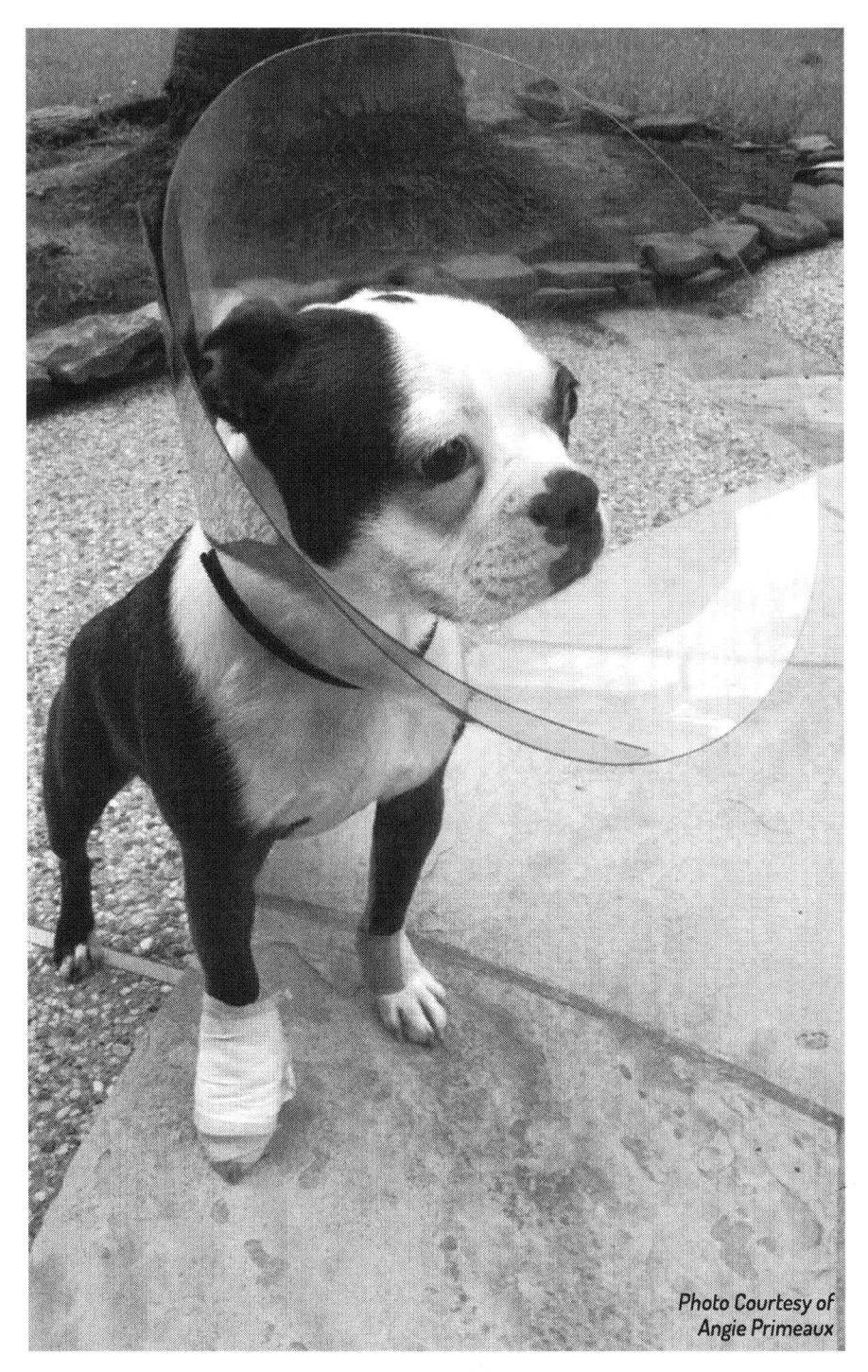

Photo Courtesy of Angie Primeaux

- Lethargy
- Seizures

Take your dog to the vet if you notice any of these issues.

Never use any product designed for a dog on a cat or vice versa. If your dog is sick, pregnant, or nursing, you may need to look for an alternative treatment. Flea collars are generally not recommended because they are known to cause problems in pets and people. If you have a cat or young children, you should choose one of the other options for keeping fleas and ticks off of your dog. This is because flea collars contain an ingredient that is lethal to felines and which is believed might be carcinogenic to humans.

When you purchase a flea treatment, make sure to read the packaging to find out when is the right time to begin treating your dog based on his current age and size. Different brands have different recommendations, and you don't want to start treating your puppy too early. There are also very important steps to apply the treatment. Make sure you understand all of the steps before you purchase the flea treatment.

If you want to use natural products instead of chemical ones, set aside a few hours to research the alternatives and find out what works best for your Boston Terrier. Verify that any natural products work before you buy them and make sure you consult with your vet. Establishing a regular schedule and adding it to the calendar will help you remember to consistently treat your dog each month.

Parasitic Worms

Although worms are a less common problem than fleas and ticks, they can be far more dangerous. Your dog can become sick from worms that are carried by fleas and ticks. There are a number of types of worms that you should be aware of:

- Heartworms
- Hookworms
- Roundworms
- Tapeworms
- Whipworms

Unfortunately, there isn't an easy-to-recognize set of symptoms to help identify when your dog has worms. However, you can keep an eye out for these symptoms, and if your dog shows them, schedule a visit to the vet.

- Your Boston Terrier is unexpectedly lethargic for at least a few days.
- Patches of fur begin to fall out (this will be noticeable if you brush your Boston Terrier regularly) or if you notice patchy spaces in your dog's coat.
- Your dog's stomach becomes distended (expands) and looks like a potbelly.
- Your Boston Terrier begins coughing, vomiting, has diarrhea, or has a loss in appetite.

If you aren't sure about any symptom, it's always best to get to the vet as soon as possible to check.

Heartworms

Heartworms are a significant threat to your dog's health and can be deadly as they can both slow and stop blood flow. You should be actively treating your dog for heartworm protection to ensure that this parasite does not have a home in your dog.

Fortunately, heartworms are among the easiest health problems to prevent. There are medications that can ensure your Boston Terrier does not get heartworms. To prevent this very serious problem, you can give your dog a chewable medication, topical medicine, or you can request shots.

This particular parasite is carried by mosquitoes, which are nearly impossible to avoid in most regions of the country. Since heartworms are potentially deadly, taking preventative measures is essential.

If a dog has heartworms, the condition is costly and time-consuming to treat and cure, but it will be well worth all of the work because of how amazing the dogs are.

1. The vet will first draw blood to conduct tests, which can cost as much as $1,000.
2. Treatment will begin with some initial medications, including antibiotics and anti-inflammatory drugs.
3. Following a month of the initial medication, your vet will give your dog three shots over the course of two months.

CHAPTER 15   General Health Issues: Allergies, Parasites, And Vaccinations

From the time when the vet confirms that your dog has heartworms until he or she says your dog is clear of the parasite, you have to keep your dog calm. Your vet will tell you how best to exercise your canine during this time. Considering your Boston Terrier is likely to be energetic, this is going to be a very rough time for both you and your dog. You will need to be careful when your dog exercises because the worms are in your dog's heart, inhibiting blood flow. Therefore, getting your dog's heart pumping too much can kill him.

Treatment will continue after the shots are complete. After about 6 months, your vet will conduct another blood test to ensure that the worms are gone.

Once your dog is cleared of the parasites, you will need to be vigilant about medicating your dog against heartworms. You want to make sure that your poor little guy doesn't suffer through that again. There will be lasting damage to your dog's heart, so you will need to ensure that your dog does not over exercise.

Intestinal Worms: Hookworms, Roundworms, Tapeworms, And Whipworms

All four of these worms thrive in your dog's intestinal tract, and they get there when your dog eats something contaminated with them. The following are the most common ways that dogs ingest worms:

- Feces
- Small hosts, such as fleas, cockroaches, earthworks, and rodents
- Soil, including licking it from their fur and paws
- Contaminated water
- Mother's milk (if the mother has worms, she can pass it to young puppies when they nurse)

The following are the most common symptoms and problems caused by intestinal parasites:

- Anemia
- Blood loss
- Coughing
- Dehydration
- Diarrhea

- Large intestine inflammation
- Weight loss

If a dog rests in soil with hookworm larvae, the parasite can burrow through the canine's skin. Vets will conduct a diagnostic test to determine if your dog has this parasite. If your dog does have hookworms, your vet will prescribe a de-wormer. You should visit a doctor yourself because humans can get hookworms, too.

Roundworms are kind of like fleas in that they are very common, and at some point in their lives, most dogs have to be treated for them. They primarily eat the digested food in your dog's stomach, getting the nutrients that your dog needs. It is possible for larvae to remain in your dog even after all of the adult worms have been eradicated. Mothers can pass these larvae to their puppies. This means if you have a pregnant Boston Terrier, you will need to have her puppies periodically checked to make sure the inactive larvae aren't passed on to the puppies. The mother will also need to go through the same testing to make sure they don't make her sick. In addition to the symptoms listed above, your Boston Terrier may appear to have a potbelly. You may also see the worms in your dog's excrement or vomit.

Tapeworms are usually eaten when they are eggs, usually carried by fleas or from the feces of other animals that have tapeworms. They develop in the canine's small intestine until they are adults. Over time, parts of the tapeworm will break off and become obvious in your dog's waste, which needs to be carefully cleaned up to keep other animals from getting tapeworms. While tapeworms typically aren't fatal, they can cause weight loss while giving your dog a potbelly (depending on how big the worms grow to be in your dog's intestines).

Your vet can test your dog to see if he has tapeworms, and will prescribe a medication that you can give your dog, including chewables, tablets, or a medication you can sprinkle on your dog's food. There is a low risk of humans getting tapeworms, with kids being at the greatest risk because of the likelihood that they will play in areas where there is dog waste and then not wash their hands carefully enough afterward. It is possible to contract tapeworms if a person swallows a flea, which is possible if your dog and home have a serious infestation.

Whipworms grow in the large intestine, and in large numbers they can be fatal. Their name is indicative of their appearance, with their tails appearing thinner than the upper section. Like the other worms, you will need to have your dog tested to determine if he is sick.

Keeping up with flea treatments, making sure people pick up behind their pets, and watching to make sure your Boston Terrier doesn't eat trash

CHAPTER 15 General Health Issues: Allergies, Parasites, And Vaccinations

or animal waste are the best preventative measures to keep your dog safe from getting these parasites.

If your dog has hookworms or roundworms, these can be spread to you from your dog through skin contact. Being treated at the same time as your Boston Terrier can help stop the vicious cycle of continually switching which of you has worms.

Preventative measures against all of these worms can be included with the preventative medication for heartworms. Talk to your vet about the different options to keep your pet from suffering any of these health problems.

Vaccinating Your Boston Terrier

Vaccination schedules are almost universal for all dog breeds, including Boston Terriers. The following list can help you ensure your Boston Terrier receives the necessary shots on schedule. Make sure to add this to your calendar. As a reminder, no shots should be administered during the first vet visit. Your new dog already has enough stress with all of the changes in his life without adding illness. If your puppy is due for more shots soon after arriving at your home, that trip should be scheduled separately, once your puppy feels more comfortable in your home.

The following table provides details on which shots should be administered and when.

Timeline	Shot		
6 to 8 weeks	Bordetella Lyme	Leptospira Influenza Virus-H3N8	DHPP – First shot Influenza Virus-H3N2
10 to 12 weeks	Leptospira Lyme	DHPP – Second shot Influenza Virus-H3N8	Rabies Influenza Virus-H3N2
14 to 16 weeks	DHPP – Third shot		
Annually	Leptospira Lyme	Bordetella Influenza Virus-H3N8	Rabies Influenza Virus-H3N2
Every 3 Years	DHPP Booster	Rabies (if opted for longer duration vaccination)	

Photo Courtesy of Mikkell Johnson

CHAPTER 15   General Health Issues: Allergies, Parasites, And Vaccinations

These shots protect your dog against a range of ailments. Keep in mind that you will need to make shots an annual part of your dog's vet visits so that you can continue to keep your pup safe. If you would like to learn more about the diseases these vaccinations protect your dog from contracting, check out the Canine Journal. They provide details about the ailments and other information that can help you understand why it is so important to keep up with the shots.

Holistic Alternatives

Wanting to keep a dog from a lot of exposure to chemical treatments makes sense, and there are many good reasons why people are moving to more holistic methods. However, doing this requires a lot more research and monitoring to ensure that the methods are working – and most importantly, do not harm your dog. Unverified holistic medicines can be a waste of money, or worse, they can even be harmful to your pet.

If you decide to go with holistic medication, talk with your vet about your options. You can also seek out Boston Terrier experts to see what they recommend before you start using any methods you are interested in trying. Read what scientists have said about the medicine you are considering. There is a chance that the products you buy from a store are actually better than some holistic medications.

Make sure you are thorough in your research and that you don't take any unnecessary risks with the health of your Boston Terrier. Thins like acupuncture are popular, but these treatments don't have the same effects on dogs as they do on humans. With many sites dedicated to taking care of Boston Terriers, you can find some information on what is recommended. It is possible that something like massage therapy can do a lot to help your dog, especially as he ages. You will need to be careful though because of how many potential health problems the breed has. Follow the recommendations on the reputable Boston Terrier sites to provide the best, safest care for your dog. There is even a special type of chiropractic therapy for dogs, but you will need to be careful about finding a reputable chiropractor for your pup so that the chiropractor doesn't do more harm than good.

CHAPTER 16
Genetic Health Concerns Common To The Boston Terrier

All purebred dogs have genetic diseases, and the Boston Terrier has more than its share of those problems. This is why it is so important to research the breeder before you adopt a puppy. Good breeders offer guarantees (Chapter 3) to ensure their puppies can be returned if they have one of a particular breed's known genetic issues. To meet the requirements of these guarantees you have to know the problems and their symptoms. The sooner you start to counter any potential problems, the healthier your Boston Terrier is likely to be. Many of their problems are related to the Boston Terrier being a brachycephaly breed, which means potential problems with their respiratory system and their eyes.

Breeders should be able to provide health records in addition to any shot records and required tests. Making sure that the parents are healthy increases the likelihood that your puppy will remain healthy over the course of his entire life. However, there is still a chance that your dog will have one of these documented problems even if the parents don't, so you will still need to keep an eye on your friend.

Allergies could be a significant problem, but they are covered in Chapter 15 as they aren't considered much of a genetic issue. This chapter focuses specifically on other potential hereditary problems.

Hip And Elbow Dysplasia

Hip and elbow dysplasia is a common problem for dogs, especially those that have a history of working. A dog's diet (Chapter 12) as a puppy can help minimize problems when he becomes an adult. Both types of dysplasia are a result of the dog's hip and leg sockets being malformed and that often leads to arthritis as the improper fit damages cartilage. It isn't something that isn't visibly obvious looking at your pup, but you will be able to see it in the stiff walk that your dog adapts when the condition is causing them pain. The condition is possible to detect by the time a dog becomes an adult, using X-rays.

CHAPTER 16   Genetic Health Concerns Common To The Boston Terrier

Dysplasia is a problem that your Boston Terrier may try to hide because he won't want to slow down. Your adult dog will walk a little more stiffly, or may pant even when it's not hot. The condition usually becomes more obvious as a dog nears his golden years, similar to the way older people tend to change their gait to accommodate pain. Getting up may become more difficult as your dog ages.

While surgery is an option in severe cases, most dogs can benefit from less invasive treatment:

- Anti-inflammatory medications – talk to your vet (dogs should not have large doses of anti-inflammatory drugs on a daily basis since these can damage your dog's kidneys)
- Lower the amount of high-impact exercise your dog gets, especially on wood floors, tile, concrete, or other hard surfaces (you can move more to do things that give him exercise and keep him active without the jarring motions of walking and jogging on hard surfaces)
- Ingestible joint fluid modifiers, like glucosamine treats
- Physical therapy (such as hydrotherapy where your dog walks on a treadmill while in water), which you will need to discuss with your vet
- Weight loss (for dogs who are overweight or obese)

Hemivertebrae

Hemivertebrae is when the tailbone vertebrae has a defect. It can result in a cute, curly tail, but that is a sign of the problem. Depending on the severity and location of the defect, it can affect other parts of the spinal column. In severe cases, it can cause nerve dysfunction that results in incontinence and difficulty walking. In the worst cases, it can cause paralysis. There is no treatment or cure for it. This is one of the ailments that a good breeder can help to minimize through good tracking and breeding practices.

Photo Courtesy of Richie Reed

CHAPTER 16   Genetic Health Concerns Common To The Boston Terrier

Patellar Luxation

The Boston Terrier may suffer from patellar luxation, which is also called slipping kneecaps. When the kneecaps are not properly fitted into the sockets, the back legs may have some minor problems. In most cases, patellar luxation is not a serious issue, and it is not known to cause much pain. However, occasionally it will require surgery to fix the repeated shift of the kneecap.

If your Boston Terrier occasionally seems to be in pain when walking or cries when out running, this could be a sign of patellar luxation. Dogs tend to hold up the affected leg for a short period of time trying to relieve the pain. It can be difficult to detect unless a dog has a more severe case, particular as your dog ages.

Eye Issues

The Boston Terrier's protruding eyes are prone to problems. For the most part, the problems aren't too serious, but you should spend time checking to make sure there isn't something wrong with them. Small scratches can become something much worse if not treated.

Entropion

Entropion is when the dog's eyelids roll inward, damaging the cornea as the eyelashes scratch it. The corrective surgery that fixes this problem can cause another eye disorder, ectropion. This is when the lower eyelid droops down so that you can see the soft pink tissue under the eye. While ectropion is not a serious problem – basset hounds live with it as a natural part of their facial structure – it does increase the likelihood of eye infections.

Cherry Eye

Glandular hypertrophy, better known as cherry eye, is caused by the third eyelid becoming inflamed. When this happens, you will be able to see the eyelid as it distends outward. Although it looks horrible, it is easily treated through surgery.

Corneal Ulcers

The cornea is the clear surface part of the eye, and it has three layers. When your dog gets a scratch, abrasion, or injury on the cornea, it can cause an ulcer. If untreated, this can lead to blindness. This is not a hereditary disease, but it is a common problem with brachial dogs because of the way their eyes protrude.

Photo Courtesy of Kimberly Brown

CHAPTER 16   Genetic Health Concerns Common To The Boston Terrier

Glaucoma

A painful eye ailment, glaucoma can result in blindness if it isn't treated early. If you notice your Boston Terrier's eyes watering a lot, the cornea turning blue, or your dog squinting often, get him to the vet. These are signs that your dog is in pain, which can be difficult to notice because you get accustomed to the behavior.

You can also have your vet do an annual glaucoma screening. This will help you know that your dog is alright.

Keratitis Sicca

Better known as dry eye, Boston Terriers tend to suffer from this because of the large size of their eyes, and how they protrude. The disease makes their tear glands less productive, so their eyes are not kept as moist as they should be. This can cause your dog to have itchy eyes, which can also encourage infections. If you notice your Boston Terrier pawing at his face or rubbing it on different things around your house, take him to the vet. There are ointments that can help, but you need to discuss your options with your vet and get some help in learning how to treat your Boston Terrier's eyes.

Injuries

This condition isn't exactly hereditary, but because Boston Terriers' eyes do stand out, they are more likely to get hurt. Scratches, scrapes, and punctures are fairly common with the breed. With dry eye being a potential problem, you really need to regularly check his eyes. Also, don't let your Boston Terrier put his head out of the car window when you are driving. Bugs and objects can hurt his eyes or can dry them out. Let your dog enjoy the ride while being safely inside the car.

Fungal Ear Infections

Dogs' ears can create a dark, warm place for fungus, yeast, and bacteria to thrive. Allergies can be a major contributing factor, but all dogs are at risk for these types of infections. This is why it is absolutely essential that you do not let your dog's ears get wet during bath time, and why you must monitor his ear health. Watch for the following issues in your dog's ears:

- Colored discharge (particularly brown or bloody)
- Swelling and redness

- Crust forming on the skin of the ear flap
- Scratching at the ear or frequent shaking of the head
- Loss of hearing or balance
- Walking in circles (beyond the usual for bathroom inspections or nesting before lying down)

If you notice any of these symptoms, take your dog to the vet, even if the symptoms seem mild. There are a number of different available treatments, depending on the severity of the condition. Usually an antifungal cream will be recommended, but more serious problems (such as an infection in the middle ear) could require injections or surgery.

If your dog suffers from chronic fungal ear infections, your vet will likely recommend an ear cleaner designed to prevent the problem or a solution that will keep the area dry.

Common Owner Mistakes

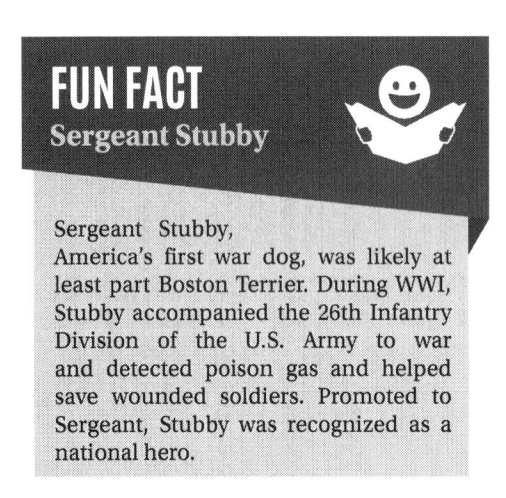

FUN FACT
Sergeant Stubby

Sergeant Stubby, America's first war dog, was likely at least part Boston Terrier. During WWI, Stubby accompanied the 26th Infantry Division of the U.S. Army to war and detected poison gas and helped save wounded soldiers. Promoted to Sergeant, Stubby was recognized as a national hero.

In addition to genetic problems, there are things that you can do that could damage your dog's health related to diet and exercise levels. In the early days, it is a difficult balance to strike as your puppy is exuberant and bouncy. Even when he is a fully grown dog, you have to make sure that you are minimizing how much stress is placed on your Boston Terrier's frame. Weight management is one important way of keeping your dog healthy. You need to ensure that your dog is getting the right nutrition for his activity level to keep him from having a greater risk of exacerbating hip and elbow dysplasia.

Failing to notice early signs of potential issues can be detrimental, even fatal. If at any point you notice strange changes in your dog's behavior, take him to the vet. As a fairly healthy breed, strange behavior in a Boston Terrier is likely a sign of something that should be checked.

CHAPTER 16   Genetic Health Concerns Common To The Boston Terrier

Prevention And Monitoring

The recent trend of "cute" overweight Boston Terriers has called attention to the potential health risks that this kind of trend can cause. This is a breed that is already cute on its own, and you should never sacrifice your dog's health in the name of cute. Instead, take extra time to train your dog to do something cute. This is both healthier and more fun for your little guy and you.

Checking your Boston Terrier's weight is important and should be done at least once a quarter or twice a year. With hip and elbow dysplasia being a real genetic problem, additional weight will only worsen things. Your vet will likely talk to you if your dog is overweight because this not only puts a strain on the dog's legs, joints, and muscles, but it can also have adverse effects on your dog's heart, blood flow, and respiratory system. Make sure to talk to your vet if you notice that your Boston Terrier is having any trouble. Those regular vet visits can help you address issues that you may not think are that big a deal. Sometimes the symptoms you notice are a sign of a future problem.

CHAPTER 17
The Aging Boston Terrier

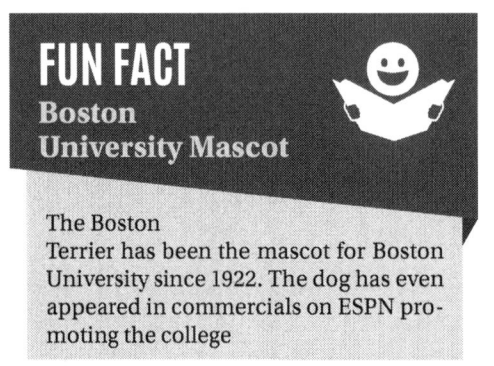

> **FUN FACT**
> **Boston University Mascot**
>
> The Boston Terrier has been the mascot for Boston University since 1922. The dog has even appeared in commercials on ESPN promoting the college

Most Boston Terriers live between 13 and 15 years, so you will probably have a number of really good years with your little gentleman or gentlewoman. A Boston Terrier that is well taken care of can live longer than that if he doesn't have many significant health issues, which makes it more all the more important to make sure your pup gets regular exercise and has a good diet. You want your Boston Terrier to live a long, happy life.

At some point you will notice that your Boston Terrier is slowing down, and that is a sign that your little buddy is starting to feel the age in his bones. This usually happens at around 9 or 10 years old. A dog may remain healthy his whole life, but his body still won't be able to do the same activities as the years start to take their toll. The changes that are necessary as your dog ages will be based on your Boston Terrier's specific needs. The first signs are usually your dog's walking becoming a little stiffer or when he starts panting more heavily earlier in the walk. If you see that, start to tone back the long walks, and just go for more, shorter walks. It's likely that your Boston Terrier will want to continue to be active, which means you will need to ensure the activity levels don't stop, just make an adjustment in the kinds of activities you do.

Your schedule is going to need to change as your canine slows down. Be careful to ensure that your pup doesn't overexert himself as Boston Terriers may be too focused on being active to realize they're hurting and need to stop to rest. Your Boston Terrier is not going to want to accept that things are changing and he won't be able to control it.

There is a reason these are called the golden years – you can really enjoy them with your dog. You don't have to worry as much about him tearing things up out of boredom or getting overexcited on walks anymore. You can enjoy lazy evenings and peaceful weekends with some less strenuous exercise to break up the day. It's easy to make the senior years incredibly enjoyable for your Boston Terrier and yourself by making the necessary adjustments.

CHAPTER 17 The Aging Boston Terrier

Photo Courtesy of Carla Flickinger

Senior Care Challenges

In most cases, caring for an older dog is much simpler than taking care of a younger dog, and Boston Terriers are no exception.

Accommodations you should make for your senior Boston Terrier include:

- Set water bowls out in a couple of different places so that your dog can easily reach them as needed.
- Cover hard floor surfaces (such as tile, hardwood, and vinyl). Use non-slip carpets or rugs.
- Add cushions and softer bedding for your Boston Terrier. This will make the surface more comfortable. There are bed warmers for dogs if your Boston Terrier displays achy joints or muscles often. Of course, you also need to make sure he isn't too warm, so this can be a fine balancing act.
- To improve his circulation, increase how often you brush your Boston Terrier.
- Stay inside in extreme heat and cold. Your Boston Terrier is somewhat hardy, but an old canine cannot handle changes in temperature as well as he once did.
- Use stairs or ramps for your Boston Terrier wherever possible so that the old pup doesn't have to try to jump.
- Avoid moving your furniture around, particularly if your Boston Terrier shows signs of having trouble with his sight or has dementia. A familiar home is more comforting and less stressful as your pet ages. If your Boston Terrier isn't able to see as clearly as he once did, keeping the home familiar will make it easier for your dog to move around without getting hurt.
- If you have stairs, consider setting up an area where your dog can stay without having to go up and down them too often.
- Create a space where your Boston Terrier can relax with fewer distractions and noises. Don't make your old friend feel isolated, but do give him a place to get away from everyone if he needs to be alone.
- Be prepared to let your dog out more often for restroom breaks.

CHAPTER 17 The Aging Boston Terrier

Photo Courtesy of Marissa Difabio

Common Physical Disorders Related To Aging

Previous chapters cover illnesses that are common or likely with a Boston Terrier, but old age tends to bring a slew of ailments that aren't particular to any one breed.

> **Here are the things you will need to watch for (as well as talking to your vet about them).**
>
> - Arthritis is probably the most common ailment in any dog breed, and the Boston Terrier is no exception. If your dog is showing signs of stiffness and pain after normal activities, talk with your vet about safe ways to help minimize the pain and discomfort of this common joint ailment.
> - Gum disease is a common issue in older dogs as well, and you should be just as vigilant about brushing his teeth when your dog gets older as at any other age. A regular check of your Boston Terrier's teeth and gums can help ensure this does not become a problem.
> - Loss of eyesight or blindness is relatively common in older dogs, just as it is in humans. Have your dog's vision checked at least once a year and more often if it is obvious that his eyesight is failing.
> - Kidney disease is a common problem in older dogs, and one that you should monitor for the older your Boston Terrier gets. If your canine is drinking more often and having accidents regularly, get your Boston Terrier to the vet as soon as possible and have him checked for kidney disease.
> - Diabetes is probably the greatest concern for a breed that loves to eat as much as your Boston Terrier does, even with daily exercise most of the dog's adult life. Although diabetes is usually thought of as a genetic condition, any Boston Terrier can become diabetic if not fed and exercised properly. This is another reason why it's so important to be careful with your Boston Terrier's diet and exercise levels.

Steps, Ramps, And Wheelchairs

You shouldn't pick your Boston Terrier up to carry him upstairs or put him in the car – he still wants to have some independence, and you could be potentially doing damage when you lift him. Steps and ramps are the best way to safely ensure your Boston Terrier can maintain some level of self-sufficiency as he ages. Also, using steps and ramps provides a bit of extra exercise.

CHAPTER 17 The Aging Boston Terrier

Photo Courtesy of Kimberly Brown

Vet Visits

As your Boston Terrier ages, you are going to notice the slow down, and the pain in your Boston Terrier's body will be obvious, just like it is in an older person. Make regular visits with your vet to ensure that you aren't doing anything that could potentially harm your Boston Terrier. If your Boston Terrier has a debilitating ailment or condition, you may want to discuss the options for ensuring a better quality of life for him, such as wheels if your Boston Terrier's legs begin to have serious issues.

The Importance Of Regular Vet Visits And What To Expect

Just as humans go to visit the doctor more often as they age, you'll need to take your dog to see your vet with greater frequency. The vet can make sure that your Boston Terrier is staying active without overdoing it, and that there is no unnecessary stress on your older dog. If your canine has sustained an injury and hidden it from you, your vet is more likely to detect it.

Your vet can also make recommendations about activities and changes to your schedule based on your Boston Terrier's physical abilities and any changes in personality. For example, if your Boston Terrier is panting more now, it could be a sign of pain from stiffness. This could be difficult to distinguish given how much Boston Terriers pant as a rule, but if you see other signs of pain, schedule a visit with the vet. Your vet can help you determine the best way to keep your Boston Terrier happy and active during the later years.

The following are the kinds of things to expect when you go to the vet.

- Your vet is going to talk about your dog's history, even if you have visited every year. This talk is necessary to see how things have gone or if any possible problems have started to manifest themselves or have gotten worse.

- While you chat, your vet will probably conduct a complete physical examination to assess your dog's health.

- Depending on how old your dog is and the kind of health he is in, your vet may want to run different tests. The following are some of the most common tests for older dogs.

  - Arthropod-borne disease testing, which involves drawing blood and testing it for viral infections

  - Chemistry Screening for kidney, liver, and sugar evaluation

  - Complete blood count

- Fecal Flotation, which involves mixing your dog's poop with a special liquid to test for worms and other parasites
  - Heartworm testing
  - Urinalysis, which tests your dog's urine to check the health of your dog's kidneys and urinary system
- The routine wellness check that the vet has been conducting on your dog for years
- Any breed-specific tests for your aging Boston Terrier

Changes To Watch For

Keep an eye out for different signs that your dog is slowing down. This will help you to know when to adjust the setup around your home and to reduce how much your old pup is exercising.

Appetite And Nutritional Requirements

With less exercise, your dog doesn't need as many calories, which means you need to adjust your pup's diet. If you opt to feed your Boston Terrier commercial dog food, make sure you change to a senior food. Senior food is designed for the changing dietary needs of older dogs, with fewer calories and more nutrients that the older dog body needs.

If you make your Boston Terrier's food, talk to your vet and take the time to research how best to reduce calories without sacrificing taste. Your canine is going to need less fat in his food, so you may need to find something healthier that still has a lot of taste to supplement the types of foods you gave your Boston Terrier as a puppy or active adult dog.

Exercise

Since Boston Terriers are so gregarious, they are going to be just as happy with extra attention from you as they were with exercise when they were younger. If you make fewer demands, decrease the number of walks, or in any way change the routine, your senior Boston Terrier will quickly adapt to the new program. You will need to make those changes based on your dog's ability, so it's up to you to adjust the schedule and keep your Boston Terrier happily active. Shorter, more frequent walks should take care of your Boston Terrier's exercise needs, as well as helping to break up your day a little more.

Your dog will enjoy napping as much as walking, especially if he gets to cuddle with you. Sleeping beside you while you watch television or as you yourself nap is pretty much all it takes to make your older Boston Terrier content, but he still needs to exercise.

The way your Boston Terrier slows down will probably be the hardest part of watching him age. You may notice that your Boston Terrier spends more time sniffing during walks, which could be a sign that your dog is tiring. It could also be his way of acknowledging that the steady walks are a thing of the past and so he is stopping to enjoy the little things more. Stopping to smell things may now give him the excitement that he used to get by walking farther.

While you should be watching for your dog to tire, he may also let you know. If he is walking slower, looking up at you, and flopping down, that could be his way of letting you know it's time to return home. If your canine can't manage long walks, make the walks shorter and more numerous and spend more time romping around your yard or home with your buddy.

Aging And The Senses

Just like people, dogs' senses weaken as they get older. They won't hear things as well as they used to, they won't see things as clearly, and their sense of smell will weaken.

The following are some of the signs that your dog is losing at least one of his senses:

- It becomes easy to surprise or startle your dog. You need to be careful because this can make your Boston Terrier aggressive, a scary prospect even in old age. Do NOT sneak up on your old dog as this can be bad for both of you, and he deserves better than to be scared.

- Your dog may seem to ignore you because he is less responsive when you issue a command. If you have not had a problem before, your dog isn't being stubborn, he is likely losing his hearing.

- Cloudy eyes may be a sign of loss of sight, though it does not mean that your dog is blind.

If your dog seems to be "behaving badly," it is a sign that he is aging, not that he doesn't care or wants to rebel. Do not punish your older dog.

Adjust your schedule to meet your dog's changing abilities. Adjust his water bowl height, refrain from rearranging rooms, and pet your dog more often. Make sure that his bed is as fluffy as when you first got it, or you can get him a new bed. Do make sure to put the bed on the ground if it was previously kept on furniture. He is probably nervous about losing his abilities, so it is up to you to comfort him.

Keeping Your Senior Dog Mentally Active

Just because your Boston Terrier can't walk as far doesn't mean that his brain isn't just as focused and capable. In fact, the changes in his body will probably be frustrating for him, so you want to make sure he has plenty of other things to keep him active and happy. As he slows down physically, focus more on activities that are mentally stimulating. As long as your Boston Terrier has all of the basics down, you can teach him all kinds of low-impact tricks. At this point, training could be easier because your Boston Terrier has learned to focus better and he'll be happy to have something he can still do with you. New toys are another great way to help keep your dog's mind active. Be careful that the toys aren't too rough on your dog's older jaw and teeth. Tug of war may be a game of the past (you don't want to hurt old teeth), but other games such as hide and seek will still be very much appreciated. Whether you hide toys or yourself, this can be a game that keeps your Boston Terrier guessing. There are also food balls, puzzles, and other games that focus on cognitive abilities.

For a dog like the Boston Terrier, additional attention and more petting are more than enough to make them happy when they get older. They will want to cuddle up to you and just be loved. This will make your Boston Terrier as happy as possible, though you still want to make sure that your dog gets some physical and mental exercise regularly too.

Some senior dogs suffer from cognitive dysfunction (CCD) syndrome, a type of dementia. It is estimated that 85% of all cases of dementia in dogs go undiagnosed because of how difficult it is to pinpoint the problem. It manifests itself more as a problem of temperament.

If your dog begins to act differently, you should take him to the vet to see if he has CCD. While there really isn't any treatment for it, your vet can recommend things you can do to help your dog. Things like rearranging the rooms of your home are strongly discouraged as familiarity with his surroundings will help your dog feel more comfortable and will reduce stress as he loses his cognitive abilities. Mental stimulation will help to fight CCD, but you should plan to keep your dog mentally stimulated regardless of whether or not he exhibits symptoms of dementia.

> **FUN FACT**
> **Judge and Gyp**
>
> The first dogs used to create the Boston Terrier breed were Judge, a cross between a Bulldog and the now-extinct white English Terrier, and Gyp, a small white dog. Their offspring were used to create a line of fighting dogs.

Advantages To The Senior Years

The last years of your Boston Terrier's life can be just as enjoyable (if not more so) than the earlier stages since your dog has mellowed. All of those high-energy activities will give way to cuddles and relaxing. Having your pup just enjoy your company can be incredibly nice (just remember to keep up with some of his activity levels instead of getting too complacent with your Boston Terrier's newfound love of resting and relaxing).

Your Boston Terrier will continue to be a loving companion, interacting with you at every opportunity – that does not change with age. Your canine's limitations should dictate interactions and activities. If you are busy, make sure you schedule time with your Boston Terrier to do things that are within those limitations. It is just as easy to make an older Boston Terrier happy as it is with a young one, and it is easier on you since relaxing is more essential to your old friend.

Preparing To Say Goodbye

This is something that no pet parent wants to think about, but as you watch your Boston Terrier slow down, you will know that your time with your sweet pup is coming to an end. Some dogs tend to suddenly decline, making it very obvious when you need to start taking extra care of their aging bodies. They have trouble on smoother surfaces or can't walk nearly as far as they once did. It's certainly sad, but when it starts to happen, you know it is time to begin to prepare to say goodbye.

Some dogs can continue to live for years after they begin to slow down, but many dogs don't make it more than about a year or two. Sometimes dogs will lose their interest in eating, will have a stroke, or other problem that arises with little warning. Eventually, it will be time to say goodbye, whether at home or at the vet's. You need to be prepared, and that is exactly why you should be making the most of these last few years.

Talk to your family about how you will care for your dog over the last few years or months of his life. Many dogs will be perfectly happy, despite their limited abilities. Some may begin to have problems controlling their bowel movements, while others may have problems getting up from a prone position. There are solutions to all of these problems. It is key to remember that quality of life should be the primary consideration, and since your dog cannot tell you how he feels, you will have to take cues from your dog. If your dog still seems happy, there is no reason to euthanize him.

CHAPTER 17   The Aging Boston Terrier

At this stage, your dog is probably very happy just sleeping near you for 18 hours a day. That is perfectly fine as long as he still gets excited about walking, eating, and being petted. The purpose of euthanasia is to reduce suffering, not to make things more convenient for yourself. This is what makes the decision so difficult, but your dog's behavior should be a fairly good indicator of how he is feeling. Here are some other things to watch to help you evaluate your dog's quality of life:

- Appetite
- Drinking
- Urinating and defecation
- Pain (noted by excessive panting)
- Stress levels
- Desire to be active or with family (if your dog wants to be alone most of the time, that is usually a sign that he is trying to be alone for the end)

Talk to your vet if your dog has a serious illness to determine what the best path forward is. They can provide the best information on the quality of your dog's life and how long your dog is likely to live with the disease or ailment.

If your dog gets to the point when you know that he is no longer happy, he can't move around, or he has a fatal illness, it is probably time to say goodbye. This is a decision that should be made as a family, always putting the dog's needs and quality of life first. If you decide it is time to say goodbye, determine who will be present at the end.

Once at the vet's office, if you have decided to euthanize the dog, you can make the last few minutes very happy by feeding your dog the things that he couldn't eat before. Things like chocolate and grapes can put a smile on his face for the remaining time he has.

You can also have your dog euthanized at home. If you decide to request a vet to come to your home, be prepared for additional charges for the home visit. You also need to determine where you want your dog to be, whether inside or outside, and in which room if you decide to do it inside.

Make sure at least one person he knows well is present so that your dog is not alone during the last few minutes of his life. You don't want your dog to die surrounded by strangers. The process is fairly peaceful, but your dog will probably be a little stressed. He will pass within a few minutes of the injection. Continue to talk to him as his brain will continue to work even after his eyes close.

Once your dog is gone, you need to determine what to do with the body.

- Cremation is one of the most common ways of taking care of the body. You can get an urn or request a container to scatter your dog's ashes over his favorite places. Make sure you don't dump his ashes in places where that is not permitted. Private cremation is more expensive than communal cremation, but it means that the only ashes you get are from your dog. Communal creation occurs when several pets are cremated together.

- Burial is the easiest method if you have your pet euthanized at home, but you need to check your local regulations to ensure that you can bury your dog at home because this is illegal in some places. You also need to consider the soil. If your yard is rocky or sandy, that will create problems with trying to bury your pet at home. Also, don't bury your pet in your yard if it is near wells that people use as a drinking source, or if it is near wetlands or waterways. Your dog's body can contaminate the water as it decays. You can also look into a pet cemetery if there is one in your area.

Grief And Healing

Dogs become members of our families, so their passing can be incredibly difficult. People go through all of the same emotions and feelings of loss with a dog as they do with close friends and family. The absence of that presence in your life is jarring, especially with such a loving, loyal dog like the Boston Terrier. It will feel weird not to have that little presence snorting along behind you as you move around your home. Just as painful, your home is a constant reminder of the loss, and in the beginning you and your family will probably feel considerable grief. Saying goodbye is going to be difficult. Taking a couple of days off work is not a bad idea. While people who don't have dogs will say that your Boston Terrier was just a dog, you know better, and it is okay to feel the pain and to grieve like you would for any lost loved one.

Losing your Boston Terrier is also going to make a substantial change in your schedule. It will likely take a while to get accustomed to the way your day-to-day life has shifted. Fight the urge to go out and get a new dog because you almost certainly are not ready yet.

Everyone grieves differently, so you will need to allow yourself to grieve in a way that is healthy for you. Everyone in your family will feel the loss differently too, so let them feel it their own ways. Some people don't require

CHAPTER 17 The Aging Boston Terrier

much time, while others can feel the loss for months. There is no timetable, so don't try to force it on yourself or any member of your family.

Talk about how you would like to remember your pup, and make sure to listen. You can have a memorial for your lost pet, tell stories, and plant a tree in your dog's memory. If someone doesn't want to participate, that is fine.

Try to return to your normal routine as much as possible if you have other pets. This can be both painful and helpful as your other pets will still need you just as much (especially other dogs who have also lost their companion).

If you find that grief is hindering your ability to function normally, seek professional help. If needed, you can go online to find support groups in your area to help you and your family, especially if this was your first dog. Sometimes it helps to talk about the loss so that you can start to heal.

Printed in Great Britain
by Amazon